1,234 QI FACTS

John Lloyd CBE is the creator of QI
and the man who devised *The News Quiz*
and *To the Manor Born* for radio and
Not the Nine O'Clock News, *Spitting Image*
and *Blackadder* for television.
His favourite page is 239.

John Mitchinson, QI's Director of Research,
has been both bookseller and publisher
and looked after authors as diverse as
Haruki Murakami, The Beatles and
a woman who knitted with dog hair.
His favourite page is 195.

James Harkin, QI's Senior Researcher,
has a maths and physics degree, a dark past
as an accountant for a chain of pubs and is
nicknamed 'Turbo' for his phenomenal work rate.
His favourite page is 2.

A QUITE INTERESTING BOOK

1,234 QI FACTS

TO LEAVE YOU SPEECHLESS

Compiled by
John Lloyd, John Mitchinson
& James Harkin

with the QI Elves
Anne Miller, Andrew Hunter Murray,
Anna Ptaszynski, Dan Schreiber
& Alex Bell

FABER & FABER

First published in 2015
by Faber & Faber Ltd
Bloomsbury House
74–77 Great Russell Street
London WC1B 3DA

Typeset by Ian Bahrami
Printed and bound in England by CPI Group (UK) Ltd,
Croydon CR0 4YY

The right of QI Ltd to be identified as author of this work
has been asserted in accordance with Section 77 of
the Copyright, Designs and Patents Act 1988

A CIP record for this book
is available from the British Library

ISBN 978–0–571–32668–6

2 4 6 8 10 9 7 5 3 1

Contents

[v]

Introduction

The world is made up of facts, not things.
LUDWIG WITTGENSTEIN

The word 'fact' has a curious history.

When it first appeared in English in the early 15th century, it had a quite different meaning to the one we use today. It came from the Latin *facere*, 'to do or make', and meant 'something done' – a 'deed' or 'act'. And, for the first hundred years of its existence, it carried mostly negative connotations.

As 'silly' once meant 'holy' and 'bully' meant 'sweetheart', 'facts' weren't so much true as bad. The world, the truth and particularly the language is in flux

everywhere. Today, we use 'fact' as a
signifier of truth – something that has
actually occurred – but, as keen viewers
of *QI* will know, even the best facts often
don't last for ever.

A hundred years from now, the fact that
a footballer is three times more likely to
be bitten by Luis Suárez than by a snake
will be meaningless, and no one will care
that four times as many babies were named
Walter because of *Breaking Bad*.

On the other hand, it's likely that bees
will continue to have five eyes.

And you still won't be able to hum and
whistle at the same time.

For us, facts like these are the currency
of wonder, the small change that opens the
turnstile between the everyday world and
the wild and mysterious universe beyond.

Fare forward, traveller – and wrap up

well! The wind coming from the centre of
the Milky Way is travelling at two million
mph . . .

JOHN LLOYD, JOHN MITCHINSON

& JAMES HARKIN

A fact is an Epiphany of God and on every fact of his life man should rear a temple of wonder and joy.

RALPH WALDO EMERSON (1803–82)

The Big Bang
was quieter than
a Motörhead concert.

The astronomer
who coined the term
'Big Bang' didn't
believe in it.

The scientist who
analysed the plutonium for
the first atomic bomb was
called Mr Doom.

The president of the
World Chess Federation
believes that, unless we play
more chess, the world
will be destroyed
by aliens.

The world champion
of French Scrabble
doesn't speak
French.

There are 19 languages
on Earth with only
one speaker left.

There are
at least 17 types of ice,
but only one exists outside
the laboratory.

Firefighters
add a 'wetting agent' to
make their water
even wetter.

It takes 50 glasses of water
to grow the oranges to make
one glass of orange juice.

Orange skin
caused by eating
too many carrots is called
carotenemia.

If you plant an apple pip,
the new tree will bear apples
that are completely different to
the one the pip came from.

Some mushrooms
have 28,000
sexes.

Magic mushrooms
grow in the gardens of
Buckingham Palace.

When the Queen gave
birth to Prince Charles,
Prince Philip was
playing squash.

Table tennis was
banned in the USSR
from 1930 to 1950 on
the grounds that it
was harmful to
people's eyes.

Wearing white at
Wimbledon began as a
way of hiding the fact
that women sweat.

The British men
most likely to wear
pink boxer shorts
live in London.

The average
British nurse eats
six free chocolates a day.

The 'Radio Nurse'
was the first baby monitor.
It came with a matching transmitter
called the 'Guardian Ear'.

The founder
of the *Daily Mail* was
convinced that Belgians
were poisoning his
ice cream.

In 19th-century London,
fake ice cream was made from
mashed turnip.

In 2014,
a Birmingham woman
phoned 999 because her
ice cream didn't have enough
sprinkles on it.

To test what happens if
someone sits on their phone,
Samsung has a robot
shaped like a
bottom.

Between 2003 and 2015,
9,000 Americans lost fingers
in snowblower
accidents.

Two-thirds of all the
people killed by volcanoes
lived in Indonesia.

Most Indonesians
speak Indonesian as a
second language.

Kim Jong-un is the
only person in North Korea
called Kim Jong-un.

The pseudonyms of
Benjamin Franklin included
Silence Dogood, Anthony Afterwit,
Alice Addertongue, Harry Meanwell,
Martha Careful, Busy Body
and Richard Saunders.

The four most
common first names among
New York City taxi drivers are
Mohammad, Mohammed,
Muhammad and Mohamed.

Not a single car
was sold by Buzz Aldrin
in the six months he worked as
a car salesman on his return
from the Moon.

Neil Armstrong
once sued his barber
for selling a lock
of his hair.

In May 2014,
the Moon had faster broadband
than most of rural Britain.

More people work for
the Chinese government
monitoring the Internet
than serve in its
armed forces.

There are four million
songs on Spotify that have
never been played.

In 2009,
92% of songs
in the *Billboard* Top 100 had
'reproductive themes'.

At any given time,
50% of 'sexters' are lying
about what they
are doing.

On average, people are
two inches shorter and
20% poorer than they
claim to be online.

Half of your anecdotes
are stolen from
someone else.

A blue whale can
swallow half a million calories
in a single mouthful.

The world champion jockey
Laffit Pincay Jr
kept his weight down by
eating half a peanut for lunch.

In 1923,
jockey Frank Hayes
won a race despite being
dead.

In 1937
at Romford dog track
you could watch cheetah racing.

Kaiser Wilhelm II
loved riding so much he
sat at his desk astride a saddle.
He said it helped him
think more clearly.

Sir Walter Scott's
salt cellar was made from
a neck bone belonging to
King Charles I.

Albert Einstein's eyeballs
are in a safety deposit box
in New York.

A newborn baby can't see
the expression on your face
if you're more than
12 inches away.

Blue whales
don't know they're blue.
They can only see in
black and white.

Composer Eric Satie
only ate white food.

For 42,000 years,
humans used cow's milk
to paint with before
anyone thought
to drink it.

A glass of cow's milk
has twice as much solid content
as a tomato.

Female kangaroos can
produce full-fat and skimmed milk
simultaneously.

Dolphin's milk
is as thick as
toothpaste.

Chalk
is made from
algae.

Birmingham University
sits on top of a mile
of fake coal mine.

The M96 is
a fake motorway
used for firefighting
practice.

The world's first road
built exclusively for cars
is now a cycle path.

In the late 19th century,
women cyclists were warned
they might get 'bicycle face',
giving them a jutting chin
and bulging eyes.

In 1849,
'running amok'
was an officially recognised
medical condition.

In 1495,
the Spanish mixed
lepers' blood with wine
to give to the French.

In the 16th century,
it was thought that
sitting in cow dung
cured diarrhoea.

The first-ever
fire engine was called
the 'Sucking Worm'.

In 1900,
Sir Arthur Conan Doyle caught fire
during a cricket match at Lord's.
The ball hit a box of matches
in his pocket.

In 2011,
two Iranian football players
were suspended for celebratory
bottom-patting.

In 2010,
Iran banned
mullet haircuts.

The Danish for 'mullet'
is *Bundesligahår*, meaning
'the hair of a German
football player'.

Until 1912,
goalkeepers were allowed
to handle the ball anywhere
in their own half.

Until 1882,
baseball umpires could
confer with the crowd if
they weren't sure whether
a catch had been made.

The first mini golf course
was invented for women who
weren't allowed to
play real golf.

In his 27-year reign,
Pope John Paul II took
more than 100 skiing and
mountain-climbing holidays.

The Pope
is not allowed to be
an organ donor because his body
'belongs to the whole Church'.

No one
in the UK
dies of natural causes.

Baths
kill more people
than terrorists.

Americans
wash their hands
800 billion times a year.

Newborn Spartan boys
were immediately
washed in wine.

Newborn babies can
recognise the theme tune from
their mother's favourite
soap opera.

Alex Salmond
once appeared in
a Bollywood soap opera.

In 2014,
more bets were placed on
who killed Lucy Beale in *EastEnders*
than on the Champions
League final.

The winning goal in the
first-ever World Cup final
was scored by a
one-armed man.

Neanderthals
took care of their
old and disabled.

Early humans
first caught bedbugs
from sharing caves
with bats.

During the Second World War,
15,000 people lived in
caves in Kent.

15,000 years ago,
cannibalism was practised
in Somerset.

The world's first powered flight
took place in Chard,
Somerset, in 1848.

The Wright brothers
only flew together once.
Their father forbade it
in case they crashed.

Immediately after
the Wright brothers' first flight,
a gust of wind flipped their plane over
and broke it.

The wind coming from
the centre of the Milky Way
is travelling at two million mph.

At 60 mph,
most of the noise a car makes
comes from contact with the road,
not from the engine.

The M25 was
so popular when it opened
that people from Norfolk
booked bus rides
around it.

In 2011,
a pensioner spent 30 hours
driving around the M25
after missing his turning.

In 1992,
a group of French youths
removing graffiti from a cave
accidentally erased a painting
of a bison that was
15,000 years old.

Medical error
is the third-largest killer of
patients in US hospitals.

Newspapers
correct fewer than 2%
of their mistakes.

Until 1922, you could listen to
the news by telephone.

The oldest person in history was
born the year Alexander Graham Bell
made the first sound transmission
and died the year that Puff Daddy
had his UK No. 1 hit
'I'll Be Missing You'.

The world's oldest land animal is a
183-year-old giant tortoise called
Jonathan. When Queen Victoria
came to the throne, he
was five years old.

In 2008,
the National Toy Hall of Fame
gave its 'Oldest Toy' award
to the stick.

The ancient Greeks
played with
yo-yos.

Twister
was originally called
'King's Footsie'.

The Chinese for
shuffling Mah Jong tiles
translates as the
'twittering of the sparrows'.

Verbs in the Archi language
of southern Russia can take
1,502,839 possible forms.

In 2001,
Saudi Arabia
banned Pokémon
for 'promoting Zionism'.

Saudi Arabia
imports camels
from Australia.

Building on sand
illegally exported from
Malaysia and Indonesia,
Singapore has expanded by
20% since the 1960s.

Since the 1930s,
American turkeys
have more than
doubled in size.

When male turkeys
see female turkeys,
they blush.

In the Middle Ages,
strapping a live chicken
to the body was thought
to cure plague.

Soldiers in Iraq
deployed live chickens to warn
of possible chemical attacks.
This was known as Operation
Kuwaiti Field Chicken (KFC).

The last McDonald's burger
in Iceland was sold in 2009,
but it can still be watched
decomposing on a webcam.

The Icelandic word
for 'pager' translates as
'thief of the peace'.

The Icelandic word
for 'computer' translates as
'number prophetess'.

Arthur Schoebius,
inventor of the Enigma machine,
also invented an
electric pillow.

The first search engine was
called Archie and was built in 1989
by a man who hasn't owned
a computer since 1983.

In 2010,
the US military
built a supercomputer
out of 1,760 PlayStation 3s.

After winning
the US quiz show *Jeopardy*,
the IBM supercomputer 'Watson'
went back to work in healthcare.

Mary Shelley kept
Percy Shelley's heart
wrapped in a poem for
30 years after his death.

In 2008,
the 18th-century German poet
Friedrich Schiller was sent
two reminders to pay
his TV licence.

Abraham Lincoln
was a licensed bartender.

Rod Stewart lost his job as
a wallpaper designer
because he was
colour-blind.

Vladimir Putin's grandfather
worked as a chef for
Stalin and Lenin,
and Rasputin.

Oliver Twist was modelled on
Butch Cassidy's grandfather.

Davros from *Doctor Who*
and Professor Yaffle from *Bagpuss*
were both based on the philosopher
Bertrand Russell.

The translation of
Harry Potter and the Philosopher's Stone
into ancient Greek is the longest
ancient Greek text produced
since AD 3.

The doctor who
administered enemas to
ancient Egyptian pharaohs was
called the 'shepherd of the royal anus'.

Box jellyfish
have 64 anuses.

Battery hens
were invented by
the ancient Romans.

In ancient Sumeria,
the laws of civilisation
and the universe were
called 'meh'.

It's against the law
in the US to own
golden eagle
feathers.

In 2014,
a man in the Italian town of Bra
was arrested for
stealing bras.

In Thailand,
the National Office of Buddhism
has a hotline for complaints
about unruly monks.

The blast furnace, the @ sign,
pretzels and genetics were
all invented by monks.

In the 15th century,
a biting epidemic swept through
the nunneries of Germany,
Holland and Rome.

Gorillas are vegetarians
but their bite is
twice as powerful
as a lion's.

Frankenstein's monster
was a vegetarian.

8 out of 10
UK vegetarians
will end up eating meat.

Finnish budget meatballs
have so little meat in them
they have had to be
renamed
'balls'.

The average supermarket
contains enough food to
keep you alive for 55 years,
or 63 years if you don't mind
eating pet food.

At least
18 species of spider
catch and eat
fish.

The world's largest spider
weighs as much as
seven bags of
crisps.

Filmgoers
eat 55% more popcorn
watching a sad film
than a comedy.

In Chile,
popcorn is called
cabritas, or 'little goats',
because of the way it
jumps in the pan.

One billion chicken wings,
five million pounds of pretzels and
four million pounds of popcorn are
eaten on Super Bowl Sunday.

Guantanamo Bay
has a gift shop.

Almost half of American adults
think that dinosaurs and
humans coexisted.

There is one
divorce in the US
every 36 seconds.

People are more likely to
believe in global warming if
you ask them in a room
containing a dead plant.

Talking to someone while
holding a warm cup of coffee
makes you more likely to think
of them as a warm person.

You're more likely to
catch a cold by holding hands
with someone than by
kissing them.

People who earn
over £75,000 a year are
more likely to believe that
stress at work is causing
their hair to fall out.

According to Fijian tradition,
the larger a woman's hair,
the more beautiful she is.

After the Chinese Manchu dynasty
conquered the Han people,
they made all the males
wear pigtails.

The hairs
on a raspberry are
its female parts.

Glow-worms
are female fireflies.

A female butterfly
has a second stomach
attached to her vagina.

The horn of the dung beetle
Onthophagus raffrayi
is more than twice the
length of its body.

A colossal squid
swallows through
its brain.

The movements
of octopuses have
no rhythm.

When people sing
together in a choir,
their heartbeats
synchronise.

The man with
the world's deepest voice
can make sounds that only
elephants can hear.

The worse a male
ring-tailed lemur smells,
the more offspring
he will have.

Male scorpionflies
use their penises to
swat away spiders.

More than
300 species of spider
pretend to be ants.

Agatha Christie was
still speaking to imaginary friends
well into her seventies.

Danish people
rate Santa Claus as more friendly
and more reliable than
most doctors.

Kurt Cobain
addressed his suicide note
to his imaginary friend,
Boddah.

Kurt Cobain's
first band was called
Fecal Matter.

The faeces of Americans
are a much less diverse ecosystem
for bacteria than those of
Papua New Guineans.

There are more bacteria on Earth
than there are stars in the
known universe.

There are more bacteria
in your armpit than there are
people in the world.

Dogs can
smell floating whale poo
from a mile away.

Camels can
open and close
their nostrils.

Astronauts' eyes
get flatter in space.

Bees
have five eyes.

Mumps
is five times
as contagious as
Ebola.

5% of
Ethiopian
epauletted fruit bats
have the Ebola virus.

In the US in 2014,
there were ten times
as many cases of measles as
there were for the entire
decade 2001–10.

A third of
all the computers in the world
contain at least
one virus.

Uzbekistan shuts down the Internet
during the nation's standardised
annual university entrance exam,
and disables all text messaging.

In the 1850s,
the entrance exam for the Royal Navy
involved writing out the Lord's Prayer
and jumping over a chair naked.

In 1853,
the *Venus de Milo* was
put on trial for nudity
in Germany.

In 2012,
a law banning nudity
in San Francisco was proposed
by a politician called
Scott Wiener.

From 1784 to 1830,
the Tory MP for Devon was
called John Bastard.

The world's biggest drilling machine
is called Bertha.

The 192nd
most powerful supercomputer
in the world is
called Gordon.

There are 299 places in Iran
called Mohammadabad.

There are craters on Mars
called Bristol, Corby, Crewe,
Tooting and Woking.

Mars is
more accurately mapped
than Alaska.

Thanks to the US military,
the most accurately mapped
country in the world
is Afghanistan.

In 2010,
the British Army parachuted
spy dogs into Afghanistan
to flush out insurgents.

The first cow to
fly in an aeroplane was
Elm Farm Ollie in 1930.
Her handler milked her and
parachuted cartons of milk
down to spectators below.

D. H. Lawrence
had a cow called Susan.

Cows
only have bottom teeth.

Cows make friends
and get sad when they are
separated from them.

One in 10 Britons
say they have
no close friends.

Most Britons
tell 10 lies a week.

A third of Britons
say they neither
'love' nor 'hate'
Marmite.

The British have
the best teeth of
any Western country.

Q

Every team in
North America's
National Ice Hockey league
has a team dentist.

Between 2003 and 2008,
the lost-property office of
Madame Tussauds collected
123 pairs of false teeth
and one false leg.

97% of the world's tigers
have been lost over
the past century.

Kaiser Wilhelm II
lost a valuable arms contract
by slapping the king of Bulgaria
on the bottom.

The word 'sovereign'
is from the Latin *superanus*,
meaning 'highest one'.

The first-ever children's picture book
was in Latin and had instructions
for beer brewing and
winemaking.

The most-borrowed book
from the Houses of Parliament library
is called *How Parliament Works*.

The 1981 Crosby by-election
included a real candidate called
Tarquin Fin-tim-lin-bin-whin-bim-
lim-bus-stop-F'tang-F'tang-
Ole-Biscuitbarrel.

Ian Fleming
said 'James Bond' was
the dullest name he'd
ever heard.

Lord Lucan
was once asked to
audition for James Bond.

Only 2% of actors
earn more than £20,000 a year.

Speeding fines in Finland
reflect the offender's earnings.
In 2002, a Nokia executive doing
75 kph in a 50 kph zone was
fined €116,000.

More people in the world
have mobile phones than
have flush toilets.

Harpo Marx
kept a harp in his bathroom
so he could practise while
on the lavatory.

'Jingle Bells' was
the first song played
in space.

9 out of 10
artificial Christmas trees
are made in China.

The average Father Christmas
on Christmas cards appears to be
two stone lighter than he was
10 years ago.

The first
commercial Christmas card
featured a drawing of a toddler
drinking a glass of wine.

In 2014,
a brewer from Virginia made a
beer from 35-million-year-old yeast.
It was described as tasting
'Belgian'.

Scottish economist
Ronald MacDonald invented the
Behavioural Equilibrium Exchange Rate,
known by the acronym 'BEER'.

Ⓠ

In Japan,
McDonald's is pronounced
makudonarudo.

There is a city in Japan
called Obama.

In Japan,
bushusuru ('to Bush') means 'to vomit'
after George Bush Sr vomited in
the Japanese PM's lap in 1992.

Japan
is home to
5.52 million vending machines.

The Infantograph,
a machine that predicts
what a couple's baby will look like,
was invented by Dr Seuss.

Irresistibubble,
the strapline for Aero,
was coined by Salman Rushdie.

Before he invented television,
John Logie Baird invented
the Baird Undersock to
combat trench foot.

Glitter was
invented by accident
by a cattle rancher from
New Jersey.

Manet's son Leon
may in fact have been his half-brother
because his wife Suzanne had
an affair with his father.

Francis and Mary Huntrodd were
both born on 19 September 1600.
They got married on their birthday
and died on 19 September 1680,
within five hours of each other.

Leonard 'Live Forever' Jones
was an American politician who
claimed he'd achieved immortality
through clean living.
He died in 1868, aged 71.

No US president
has ever died
in May.

There are more porn sites
hosted in the US
than there are people
in the US.

There are more people on
America's 'suspected terrorist' list
than live in the whole
of Estonia.

Americans eat
350 slices of pizza
every second.

The atmosphere of Venus
is so hot it would cook a
pizza in seven seconds.

In 2013,
after six months monitoring
two suspected Chinese spy drones
invading their airspace, the
Indian army discovered
they were Jupiter
and Venus.

In Florida in 2012,
a woman called Crystal Methany
was arrested for drug possession.

In 2011, the Chinese military
tried to pass off a scene from *Top Gun*
as footage of its own air force.

In 2010,
a doctor in Blackpool spent £1,200
trying to win a giant cuddly toy
at a hoopla stall.

The all-time fastest-selling
Playmobil figure, issued in 2015,
is Martin Luther, complete with
quill pen and German Bible.

The American version of
Meccano is called
Erector.

Pixar
accidentally deleted *Toy Story 2*
halfway through making it.

Keira Knightley's
first name is a spelling mistake
by her mother.

Most US pop songs
are written for people
with a reading age of nine.

The real name
of the rapper Akon
is Aliaune Damala Bouga Time
Bongo Puru Nacka Lu Lu Lu
Badara Akon Thiam.

'Waterloo Sunset', by the Kinks,
was originally called
'Liverpool Sunset'.

The theme tune for
Desert Island Discs was
inspired by the view over
Bognor Regis.

The world's oldest
footprints outside Africa
were found on a beach
in Norfolk.

The world's oldest spider's web
was found in amber in
East Sussex.

The world's most complete
fossil of a Tyrannosaurus rex
has its teeth wrapped round
the most complete fossil
of a triceratops.

When the dinosaurs were alive,
there were active volcanoes
on the Moon.

A restaurant in Lanzarote
cooks its food using the heat
from a volcano.

The Shredded Wheat company
once had a restaurant offering
Shredded Wheat ice cream
and roast turkey served with
Shredded Wheat stuffing.

The Tlatelcomila cannibals
of ancient Mexico ate human flesh
with chilli sauce.

The American criminal
known as 'the Swiss Cheese Pervert'
for having sex covered in cheese
is from Philadelphia.

Uncle Ben's rice
was invented in Britain
by a German chemist.

Ninjas sent
secret messages using
coloured grains of rice.

British war censors
found James Joyce's book *Ulysses*
so difficult to read that they
were convinced it was
written in code.

The world's most successful hacker
was himself hacked and arrested
because his password was
his cat's name
plus '123'.

The underwater cable
that powers the Internet
in Southeast Asia is
being eaten by sharks.

One in six dolphins
in the Bahamas have been
bitten by a shark.

The word
'Godzilla' means
'Gorilla-Whale'.

A crayfish can
grow new brain cells
from its blood cells.

Penguins
can't taste fish.

Catfish
hunt pigeons.

Owls
sunbathe.

Dolphins
can't sneeze.

Because there are
10 billion trillion nematode worms,
the vast majority of animals
don't have legs.

The oldest known
snake fossil had
four feet.

Some male spiders have
special legs designed to hold
females' jaws open during sex
so they don't get eaten.

Carib cannibals
slit the legs of their victims
and ate them stuffed
with pimientos.

Before the
invention of anaesthesia,
amputating a leg took
under a minute.

Smokers are
16 times more likely to
have a limb amputated
than non-smokers.

Pez dispensers are
shaped like cigarette lighters
because they were designed
to help stop smoking.

Four of the six
'Marlboro men' have died
of smoking-related
diseases.

The music on the
anti-piracy advert used
on all DVDs was
itself pirated.

10% of all the food
stolen in Italy in 2006
was Parmesan.

1.5 million trolleys are
stolen from British supermarkets
every year.

You could fit
all 3,561 Tesco stores in the UK
into an area the size of
the City of London.

The 65 square miles
of northern France that are
still uninhabitable after the
First World War will take
300 years to make safe.

In the last 500 years,
a third of the floods in the
southern Netherlands were created
by humans as weapons of war.

All the American war dead
on European soil were buried
facing away from Germany,
apart from George S. Patton,
who is facing his troops.

Every hour,
one US war veteran
commits suicide.

In the month after
Marilyn Monroe killed herself,
there was a 12% jump in
the US suicide rate.

At least one in 10 people
in the Stone Age were murdered,
compared to one in 100,000 today.

Neanderthals
hunted and ate
pigeons.

Bhutan has
an official yeti hunter.
He hasn't found any
(at least, not yeti).

In the early 2000s,
Tonga's finance minister
was also its official
court jester.

The *copreae* were
jesters in the Roman imperial court.
Their name translates as
the 'Little Shits'.

Roman slaves
had their foreheads
tattooed with the words
'Stop me, I'm a runaway.'

There are more tattoos on
British teachers than there are
on members of the British
armed services.

Henry III of France
loved the game of cup-and-ball
so much he set up schools to
teach people how to play.

Jack Nicholson
once got detention at school
every single day for a year.

US chess grandmaster
Bobby Fischer was at school
with Barbra Streisand.
She had a crush on him.

According to North Korea's
official teachers' manual,
Kim Jong-un learnt to drive
at the age of three.

In 2000,
Ushers brewery in Trowbridge
was dismantled and rebuilt
in a cabbage patch
in North Korea.

In the 1930s,
England had 3,000
dedicated ginger-beer
breweries.

In 1710,
the boys of Winchester College
rioted over inadequate
beer rations.

The state treasurer
of Alabama is called
Young Boozer.

The largest
poster ever produced
features the president and
prime minister of Turkey
and is two-thirds the size
of a football pitch.

US President James Garfield's
favourite meal was
squirrel soup.

Teddy bears
are named after President
Theodore 'Teddy' Roosevelt.

Teddy Roosevelt's sons
Theodore and Kermit
were the first Westerners to
shoot a giant panda.

A sniper
was originally someone who
shot snipe.

Merry-go-rounds
were originally a training device
for knights.

The word 'aquarium'
originally meant 'a watering place
for cattle'.

One of the names
originally proposed for Neanderthals
was *Homo stupidus*.

Humans
have shorter attention spans
than goldfish.

The average woman
deletes four selfies for
every one she's happy with.

The only person
ever killed by a boa constrictor
was an escapologist who got
into a coffin with one.

There are
six billion kinds
of knot.

The only meteorite
known to have hit a person
is called the 'Hodges Meteorite':
it slightly injured Mrs Ann Hodges
in Alabama in 1954.

Isaac Newton
walked out of the
only opera he ever attended.

Alan Shepard,
the only man to
play golf on the Moon,
missed the ball on his
first attempt.

The Ministry of Defence
owns 15 golf courses.

The US government
spends £300,000 a year
studying the body language of
other countries' leaders.

The British government
in the 1830s spent £17,000
developing a working model
of Charles Babbage's computer –
more than twice the cost of
a warship at the time.

In 1910,
France had more aeroplanes than
Germany, Britain, Italy, Russia, Japan
and the US combined.

The front between Islamic State and
the Iraqi Kurds in 2015 was 50%
longer than the Western Front in 1914.

The US military is America's
largest purchaser of explosives;
number two is Disney World.

After Disney released
The Princess and the Frog,
more than 50 children were
hospitalised with salmonella
after trying to kiss frogs.

Walt Disney
used to pack his testicles in ice
to help improve his
sperm count.

96% of sperm cells
are abnormal.

A whale's sperm cell is
about the same size
as a human one.

Starfish
breathe and smell
through their
feet.

Sniffer dogs
can be trained to find
USB sticks.

Bats' throats
contain the fastest muscles
of any mammal.

After fights,
Roman gladiators
drank vinegar mixed with ash
to help their bodies recover.

Gladiators prepared for combat
by covering themselves
with marshmallow sap.

Three members of
ITV's *Gladiators* team were
also in the film *Gladiator*.

The first pornographic movie
came out in 1895, a few months after
the first regular movie.

The Big Parade (1925) was the
first film to include a swear word.
As it was a silent movie,
the word 'damn' appeared
on a dialogue card.

In *The Exorcist*,
the sound effect of the girl's neck
ratcheting round was made by
the director twisting his
cracked leather wallet.

Airplane! was released in Germany
as *The Unbelievable Journey
in a Crazy Aeroplane.*

The Italian for 'break a leg' is
'*in culo alla balena!*' – literally
'into the arse of a whale!'

The Arabic for 'incubator'
literally translates as
'chicken machine'.

When *Fawlty Towers*
was broadcast in Spain,
Manuel became an Italian
named Paolo.

The Roman poet Catullus
claimed the Spanish used their
morning urine as
a mouthwash.

In 2015,
Islamic State threatened 80 lashes
for anyone caught watching
Real Madrid play Barcelona.

The first version of
football's offside rule stated that
players shouldn't 'loiter'
near the opposing goal.

In a game of football in 1280,
a player was killed after running
into another player's dagger.

Before they got whistles,
football referees waved
a handkerchief.

FIFA
has 18 more members
than the UN.

Until the FA banned
women's football in 1921,
it was more popular
than men's.

There are fewer women
on corporate boards in America
than there are men
named John.

If your parents
are happily married,
your risk of divorce
decreases
by 14%.

Under medieval Welsh law
women could divorce their
husbands if they had
bad breath.

On the streets of Mumbai,
you can get your ears
cleaned for
25 pence
an ear.

When the telephone was invented,
there were concerns it would create
left-eared people.

In 1969,
to protect them from noise
elephants living near Heathrow
were given ear muffs.

An elephant's sense of smell
is so good it can distinguish
between members of different
African tribes.

Dogs
investigate bad smells
with their right nostril and
good smells with their left.

The Navajo name for
Adolf Hitler translates as
'he who smells his moustache'.

Titan,
Saturn's largest moon,
smells like a mixture of
petrol and farts.

Moles
smell in stereo.

B&Q recalled its mole repellent
from Northern Irish stores in 2008
after it was pointed out there are
no moles in Ireland.

Moles can dig
at a rate equivalent to a man
shifting 3,000 shovel-loads
of earth an hour.

Mankind has reached
20 billion miles beyond the Earth
but only seven and a half
miles inside it.

A gram of soil
contains a million
different species.

Luke Skywalker's lightsaber
from *Return of the Jedi* spent
two weeks in space on the
shuttle *Discovery* in 2007.

The International Space Station is
the single most expensive
object ever built.

Three-quarters of astronauts
take sleeping pills.

South Korea shut down
its entire space programme in 2014
when its only astronaut
resigned.

The word '*bull*' means
'light bulb' in North Korea and
'testicle' in South Korea.

At their current birth rate,
there will be no South Koreans
at all by 2750.

The rate of extinction for species in
the 20th century was 100 times higher
than it would have been
without human impact.

The iceberg that hit the *Titanic*
was 3,000 years old; it formed when
Tutankhamun was pharaoh.

Tutankhamun
was the owner of all
the ancient Egyptian socks
that have survived.

The only carnivorous mouse
in North America
eats scorpions and
howls at the Moon.

Sanskrit has 40 words for 'mouse',
including '*mushka*', which means
both 'little mouse'
and 'testicle'.

Agatha Christie gave
the rights to *The Mousetrap*
to her grandson as a
birthday present.

Hercule Poirot
was described by
Agatha Christie as a 'detestable,
bombastic, tiresome, egocentric
little creep'.

Daniel Defoe
once had a job
harvesting musk from the
anal glands of cats.

T. S. Eliot
wore pale-green make-up.
Nobody knows why.

J. R. R. Tolkien and C. S. Lewis once
went to a party dressed as polar bears.
It wasn't a fancy-dress party.

If a mother polar bear fails to
double her weight during pregnancy,
the foetus is reabsorbed
into her body.

Aztec mothers
who died in childbirth
were regarded as highly as
warriors who died in battle.

The chance of two expectant
mothers with the same due date
giving birth on the same day
is one in 200.

Novercaphobia is
the fear of stepmothers.

Mother cats stimulate
their kittens to defecate by
licking their bottoms.

Being born in September
increases your chance of getting
into Oxford or Cambridge by 12%.

Stephen Hawking was born
on the 300th anniversary
of Galileo's death.

Emily Brontë, who wrote
Wuthering Heights, and Kate Bush,
who sang 'Wuthering Heights',
were both born on 30 July,
140 years apart.

One in 20
Twitter accounts is
a non-human spam bot.

Even if teleportation were possible,
there is so much data in a human being
that teleporting just one person would
take 350,000 times longer
than the age of the universe.

Saturn V,
the tallest-ever space rocket,
was taller than all but one
of the trees on Earth.

Apollo 11's
fuel consumption
was seven inches
to the gallon.

The maximum length
that a fly can grow to is
two and a half inches.

During the Second World War,
people in Okinawa read at night
using light from phosphorescent
marine animals.

In the last 200 years,
the world's oceans have absorbed
more than a quarter of the
carbon dioxide released
by humans.

There are at least
a billion tons of ice
on the Moon.

People sleep
20 minutes longer on nights
when there is a full moon.

City skies are lighter
on cloudy nights than on clear nights
(even when there is a full moon)
because the clouds reflect back
the light pollution.

Moonshine alcohol is called
'Crazy Mary' in Brazil,
'Kill me quick' in Kenya and
'Push me, I push you' in Nigeria.

If you get a zebrafish drunk,
other zebrafish will
follow it around.

Male mosquitofish
have such large penises
they can't swim straight.

The man with
the longest penis on record
is a data entry clerk
from Manhattan.

From 1994 to 2000,
Manhattan's Twins restaurant
was staffed entirely by
identical twins.

The world record
for the most people
sat on one chair
is 1,831.

The first execution
by electric chair in 1890
took eight minutes.

While St Lawrence was being
executed on a red-hot griddle,
he asked to be turned over as
'one side was perfectly cooked'.

St Simon and
St James the Less
were sawn to death.

As the hands of St Kevin
were outstretched in prayer,
a blackbird laid an egg in them,
and he stayed in that position
till it hatched.

Magpies
prefer blue items
to shiny ones.

Rats
dream about
places they want
to explore.

To stay alive,
a hummingbird needs
to eat 300 fruit flies a day.

An attempt to make
the world's biggest sandwich
in Iran failed when the crowd
ate it before it could
be measured.

There is a
renewable-energy
recruitment agency called
Earth, Wind and Hire.

One of the world's biggest
lift manufacturers is called
Schindler's Lifts.

One of the crown jewels is called
'The Pointless Sword of Mercy'
because it has its
end cut off.

The pipe tobacco
Baby's Bottom was named
for the smoothness
of its taste.

The most popular exhibit
in the Smithsonian's modern-
physics collection is
Einstein's pipe.

Darts evolved from
a game called 'puff and dart',
which was played in pubs
with a blowpipe.

During the Second World War,
Canada tested killer darts
on sheep dressed in
military uniform.

The last time an elephant
took part in battle was in 1885,
for Vietnam against France.

During the Second World War,
Japanese soldiers hid grenades inside
coconuts and used them
as weapons.

The first shot
of the First World War
was fired in Togo, West Africa.

Nigerian
email scams were
introduced to Nigeria
by the British.

When it rains heavily
in the Sumatran rainforests,
there is a corresponding drought
in East Africa, 3,700 miles away.

The Hebrew name for the film
Cloudy with a Chance of Meatballs
translates as 'It's Raining Falafel'.

J. M. Barrie
nearly called *Peter Pan*
'The Boy Who Hated Mothers'.

J. K. Rowling's
parents met at
King's Cross station.

In 1899,
Thomas and Alice Day
named their newborn son
Time Of.

In 1896,
the 937th most popular name
for a boy in the US was
Josephine.

Linus Pauling's sister
was called Pauline.

If Napoleon's sister Pauline
got cold feet, she warmed them
in the cleavage of one of
her ladies-in-waiting.

In 1454, Philip the Good held a feast
that included a lion chained to a pillar
protecting a statue of a nude woman
who served mulled wine from
her right breast.

The earliest known feast
consisted of 71 tortoises,
roasted in their shells.

The first recorded soup
dates from 10,000 BC, the first beer
from 7,000 BC and the first tortillas
from 6,000 BC.

Sweet-and-sour sauce
was eaten in medieval Britain.

Condors
sometimes eat so much
they can't take off.

Since 1972,
Don Gorske from Wisconsin
has eaten more than
26,000 Big Macs.

McDonald's
used to sell
bubble-gum-flavoured
broccoli.

To digest baobab seeds,
chimpanzees have to eat them,
pick them out of their faeces
and then eat them again.

Dog food
is used to test lavatories because
it has the same consistency
as human faeces.

Because dogs aren't allowed
at Selwyn College, Cambridge,
the Master's basset hound has been
reclassified as 'a very large cat'.

John Adams,
second president of the US,
had a dog called Satan.

Speedy Gonzalez
had a cousin called
Slowpoke Rodriguez.

There have been Britons called
Rhoda Turtle, Jesus Devilheart,
Dick Thick and Willy Cockhead.

The NYPD's crackdown on
illegal cockfighting in 2014 was
called 'Operation Angry Birds'.

Policemen in Grenada
wear their Twitter handles
on their uniforms.

As punishment for misbehaviour,
policemen in Thailand have to wear
Hello Kitty armbands.

According to the
company that created her,
Hello Kitty isn't a cat.

Cats can recognise
their owners' voices but
have evolved to
ignore them.

Every year, the Bank of England's
damaged and mutilated notes service
receives claims of over £100,000
for banknotes eaten by pets.

83% of US pet owners
refer to themselves as the
animal's 'mom' or 'dad'.

The UK spends
five times as much on pet food
as it does on baby food.

Since we domesticated dogs,
human brains have
got smaller.

The same part of your brain
lights up when you hear the words
'hammered the nail' as it does when
you actually hammer a nail.

At the turn of the 20th century,
animal brains were used
to thicken milk.

Donkey's milk
is the best natural substitute
for human breast milk.

London milkmaids
used to shout 'mi-ow' in the streets.
It was short for 'milk below'.

The arrival of cats
in North America led
to the extinction of
40 species of dog.

Snake's venom
evolved from
saliva.

A boa constrictor
monitors its victim's heart,
and stops squeezing
when it stops
beating.

The first female chief
of the Cherokee Nation was called
Wilma Mankiller.

There are American politicians called
Dick Swett, Frank Shmuck
and Butch Otter.

More Americans think
that Barack Obama is a Muslim than
accept the theory of evolution.

The area of land
seized from Native Americans
by the US since 1776 is
25 times larger than
the UK.

The most common job
in America is
truck driver.

Until 1925, drivers going east–west
in New York stopped on amber and
drove on green, but drivers going
north–south stopped on green
and drove on amber.

Since 1902, the *New York Times* has
published at least five articles
announcing the return
of the monocle.

In 1952, the Great Smog of London
was so bad that blind people led
sighted people home from
the train stations.

Due to heavy snow in 1891,
the 3 p.m. train service from
Paddington to Plymouth
left on 9 March and
arrived on 13 March.

In 2014,
not a single 07.29 a.m.
Brighton–London Victoria train
reached its destination on time.

The hands of the clock
on Bolivia's congressional building
move anticlockwise to encourage
people to think creatively.

Scientists have
performed brain surgery
on cockroaches.

80% of a cricket
is edible, compared to
40% of a cow.

64% of the diet of
cane toads is other
cane toads.

Lemon ants
taste of
lemon.

You have
taste receptors
in your anus.

Near the anus
of the horseshoe bat is
an extra pair of false nipples.
The baby bats use them
as handles to
cling to.

Bees
can fly higher
than Mount Everest.

The world's largest saw
was used to cut through
a mountain in Kazakhstan.

There are mountains in Antarctica
called Nipple Peak, Dick Peaks
and Mount Cocks.

16th-century fabric colours included
Puke, Gooseturd, Dead Spaniard
and Dying Monkey.

The word 'donkey'
used to rhyme
with 'monkey'.

The word 'fizzle'
once meant 'to fart
without making a noise'.

Fartplan
is Danish for
'timetable'.

The longest-ever Viking longship
was unearthed by accident
during renovations of
a Danish longship
museum.

The Vikings
had a god and a goddess
of skiing.

'Skull', 'slaughter', 'hell',
'weak', 'anger' and 'freckles'
are all words of
Viking origin.

The most
common inscription
found on Viking coins is
'There is no god
but Allah.'

Male coin spiders
only have sex once.
After mating, they chew off
their own genitals.

To be soft enough to chew,
the first-ever breakfast cereal
had to be soaked in
milk overnight.

Potatoes soaked in vinegar,
soda water and biscuits were what
Lord Byron lived on in his twenties.
He weighed less than nine stone.

Kanye West
hasn't smiled in photographs
since he noticed that people
in old paintings don't
smile either.

Your computer knows
more about you than
your friends and
family do.

You are
genetically more similar
to your friends than
to strangers.

The 'like' button on
the Latin version of Facebook
says *mihi placet* —
'it pleases me'.

The first item
listed on eBay was
a broken laser pointer.

Wikipedia
has a page on
'The Reliability of Wikipedia'.

The Wikipedia page for 'pedant'
has been edited more than
500 times.

Three times
as many people follow
Russell Brand on Twitter
as all 650 British MPs
combined.

The banned website
most often clicked by MPs in
the Houses of Parliament
is sexymp.co.uk.

A single human brain
has more switches than
all the computers and
Internet connections
on Earth.

A single human nose
produces about a cupful
of mucus a day.

Over 7,000 species
of plants and animals have been
cultivated for human consumption,
but just four crops – rice, wheat, corn
and potatoes – make up two-thirds
of everything we eat.

More fish are farmed every year
than pigs, sheep, cows and
chickens put together.

The consumption of chickens
in ancient Rome was restricted
to one per person
per meal.

Nando's is
the world's biggest buyer
of South African art.

The oldest human art
is spray-painted graffiti
from Indonesia.

In the Cook Islands,
online business domains
end in .co.ck

Penis worms
can turn their mouths
inside out and walk
on their throats.

Tapeworms
can cause
epilepsy.

Eating chocolate
improves your memory,
but only if you eat so much of it
that it's bad for
your health.

Smoky bacon Pringles,
prawn cocktail Walkers and
McCoy's sizzling BBQ crisps
are all suitable for vegans.

The Yorkshire village of Fryup
turned down a request by the
animal-rights charity PETA
to change its name to
Vegan Fryup.

There is a village in Russia
where every single person knows
how to tightrope walk.

23 villages in
Russia's Krasnoyarsk region are
entirely inhabited by men.

Chernobyl
will be uninhabitable
for at least 20,000 years.

The oldest known
customer-service complaint letter was
written on a clay tablet in 1750 BC.

When the first
sewing factories opened,
seamstresses complained of
'extreme genital excitement'
caused by the sewing machines.

Disney ignored the complaint
from *Mary Poppins* author P. L. Travers
that the song 'Let's Go Fly a Kite'
should be 'Let's Go *and* Fly a Kite'.

I'm a Celebrity . . . Get Me Out of Here!
gets a letter of complaint every year
from naturalist Chris Packham
about the way they
exploit animals.

A tarantula hawk
is neither a tarantula nor a hawk;
it's a giant wasp with the second
most painful insect sting
in the world.

Queen bees
lay eggs through
their stings.

Cockroaches
can hold their breath
for 40 minutes.

Dung beetles
can bury 250 times
their own weight in dung
in a single evening.

The fastest bus in the world
is powered by
cow dung.

The fastest sprinters
have very symmetrical
knees.

The best long-distance runners
have very symmetrical
nostrils.

The Yupno people
of Papua New Guinea
use their noses to point with
instead of their
fingers.

The tiny hairs in your nose
are the last things to
stop beating when
you die.

The deaths of
George I of England, Pope Paul II,
Pope Clement VII, Frederick the Great,
Maximilian I Archduke of Austria and
Albert II of Germany were all
due to melon overdose.

Szechuan peppers
make the lips
vibrate.

A kiss on the lips
can transfer 80 million bacteria
into another person's mouth
in 10 seconds.

There are
40 billion bacteria
in one gram of faeces.

To make enough faeces
to feed its larvae,
a flea has to drink
30 times its own weight
in blood.

The black legs
of Marabou storks
usually appear white because
they're covered in
excrement.

The 10,000 species of birds
alive today make up
less than 1% of all the bird species
that have ever existed.

A bird caused
the Large Hadron Collider
to be turned off in 2009 after
it dropped a piece of
baguette into it.

The 65 billion neutrinos
that pass every second through
every square centimetre of your body
were created 8.5 minutes ago
in the centre of the Sun.

No one knows why the centre of the Sun
is not nearly as hot as its surface.

The Sun rotates
around its axis every 26 days
but, because it's made of gas,
different bits rotate at
different speeds.

The Sun is
located in the Milky Way
between the third and fourth arms
of a cloud of stars known as
the Local Fluff.

The Milky Way
is corrugated.

Corrugated iron
is not made from
iron.

The Man in the Iron Mask's mask
wasn't made of iron
but velvet.

The beard of the
death mask of Tutankhamun broke off
when a light bulb in the display case
was being changed.

Inês de Castro was
proclaimed queen of Portugal in 1357,
despite dying two years earlier.

'Old person smell' is
caused by a molecule called 2-nonenal,
which increases in your body
as you age.

Penicillin was
originally called
'mould juice'.

You can smell
a flock of macaroni penguins
from six miles away.

The olive sea snake has
light sensors in its tail
so it can check that its
whole body is hidden.

Light detectors in frogs' eyes
are so sensitive that they can
detect single photons of light.

The ancient Greek cure for
cataracts was to pour
hot broken glass
into the eyes.

One in a thousand
lightning bolts are invisible
to the human eye.

You are 100 times more likely
to be struck by lightning
standing under an oak
than a beech.

In the First World War,
actor Basil Rathbone
led covert missions
disguised as
a tree.

In 1745,
King Louis XV went to
a ball dressed as a
yew tree.

The first Christmas tree in
the Vatican went up
in 1982.

In the 1670s,
the Pope bought
'St Peter's Beard' from
highwayman Dick Dudley and kissed it,
not knowing it was actually a
prostitute's pubic wig.

Only humans kiss
with tongues.

Peter Cushing
and Christopher Lee
both wore toupees.

The place where
Julius Caesar was murdered
is now a cat sanctuary.

Caligula made it
illegal on pain of death
to mention a goat
in his presence.

President Mobutu Sese Seko of Zaire
banned all leopard-print hats,
except for his own.

The Hawaiian for 'certified',
hooiaioia, has eight
consecutive
vowels.

Ulaia
is an old Hawaiian word
meaning 'to live like a hermit
because of disappointment'.

The world's last surviving
male northern white rhino
lives under 24-hour
armed guard.

In 1958,
the people of São Paulo voted
a rhino named Cacareco
onto the city council.

The town of
Dorset, Minnesota,
elects its mayor by raffle.

In 1995,
Nelson Mandela was voted
Santa Claus of the Year by
the children of Greenland.

It's more likely to snow
in the UK at Easter
than at Christmas.

Before going on stage for
public readings, Charles Dickens
drank rum, sherry and
a pint of champagne.

A Tale of Two Cities
contains the first known reference
to potato chips.

The glue that seals crisp packets
is dried instantly using
particle accelerators.

According to its website,
WD-40 was once used by police
to remove a naked burglar from
an air-conditioning vent.

In some parts
of southern Africa,
mosquito nets are
mostly used
for fishing.

The first dice were used
to tell the future.

The first bra
was made from
handkerchiefs.

In 2007,
eight-year-old twin boys from Ohio
invented wedgie-proof
underpants.

Before paint tubes were invented,
artists kept their paint
in pigs' bladders.

The first product
sold by mail order was
Welsh flannel.

From 1700 until 1905,
cows were tied to posts in
St James's Park and their milk
sold 'straight from the udder'.

The offspring of
a cow and a bison
is called a 'beefalo'.

The largest diamond ever found
comes from Brazil and
is called 'Sergio'.

The national anthem
of Bosnia and Herzegovina is called
'The National Anthem
of Bosnia and Herzegovina'.

In 2004,
Mexico fined a singer for
stumbling over the words
while singing the national anthem.

Only 2% of Belgians
know their national anthem.

Between 1910 and 1926,
Portugal had 45
governments.

The Republic of Ireland
didn't have postcodes
until 2015.

In 2000,
the Royal Mail withdrew its
sponsorship of Postman Pat,
on the grounds that he no longer
fitted its corporate image.

The 1908 London Olympics were
sponsored by Oxo, Odol mouthwash
and Indian Foot Powder.

For the first 50 years
of the ancient Greek Olympics,
the only event was the
200-metre sprint.

Due to quarantine laws,
the equestrian events at the
1956 Melbourne Olympics
took place in Stockholm.

The 1900 Paris Olympics
featured a 200m swimming race
with obstacles.

Men's underwater swimming
at the 1900 Olympics was never
held again due to 'lack of
spectator appeal'.

The javelin competition
at the 1900 Olympics
was held in a public park.
Competitors had to be
careful not to hit anyone.

The reigning
Olympic tug-of-war champions
are the City of London Police.

For the Pope's visit in 2015,
traffic police in Manila were
issued with 2,000 nappies
so they never had to
leave their posts.

Troops in
Operation Desert Storm
wore water-filled Pampers nappies
on their heads to keep cool.

In the First World War,
only Romanian officers
above the rank of major
were authorised to wear
eye shadow into battle.

In the 1930s,
a fashion craze for girls
to wear monocles swept Liverpool.

Ralph Lauren
was born
Ralph Lifshitz.

If Hitler's father
hadn't changed his surname in 1877,
the Third Reich would have been
led by Adolf Schicklgruber.

For marrying a Protestant,
Josef Goebbels became the only Nazi
to be excommunicated.

In the 5th century AD,
the Catholic Church
excommunicated
all mime artists.

Ivan the Terrible
once sewed an archbishop
into a bearskin and had him
hunted down by a pack of dogs.

Catherine the Great,
Empress of Russia,
wasn't called Catherine,
wasn't Russian and
hated being called
'the Great'.

Peter the Great
slept with a servant's stomach
for a pillow.

Hitler's plan for Moscow
was to level the city and turn it
into an enormous lake.

The sixth-
biggest river
in the world is
under the sea.

The longest canyon in the world is
50% longer than the Grand Canyon
and buried under the ice
in Greenland.

The world's largest container ship
can carry 900 million cans of
baked beans – 60 beans for
every person on Earth.

Scallops caught in Brittany
are shipped to China for cleaning
and then sent back to France
to be cooked and eaten.

In 2017,
China will open
the world's first stadium
dedicated to online gaming.

Chongqing in China
has a smartphone-only lane
for pedestrians.

92% of the
population of China is
lactose intolerant.

Only 20% of people who
think they're allergic to penicillin
actually are.

The first known case of
'Climate Change Delusion'
took place in 2008, when a man
refused to drink water as he felt guilty
about 'taking it from the Earth'.

The first occupational disease
ever recorded in medical literature
was 'chimney sweep's scrotum'.

In 19th-century Australia,
it was thought that climbing
inside a dead whale would
cure rheumatism.

Kidney donors
live longer than
the average person.

In 1800,
the average age of
an American was 16.
Today, it's 38.

When a country is
in recession,
life expectancy
goes up.

Finland
is the world's
least fragile state.

The sauna
at Helsinki airport
is unisex, and clothing
is optional.

The first passenger flight
lasted 23 minutes and flew
at an altitude of 15 feet.

In the first
BBC radio news report,
the news was read twice,
once quickly and once slowly.
Listeners were asked which
they preferred.

The first budgerigars
sold in Europe cost
as much as a house.

The first novel
was Japanese and
ended in mid-sentence.

The Japanese government's
official biography of
Emperor Hirohito
is 61 volumes long.

During the Second World War,
Churchill wore a specially designed
onesie, which he called
his 'Siren Suit'.

The first Churchill Insurance mascot
was a bulldog called Lucas who
was sacked for refusing
to hold a phone in
his mouth.

Asda holds
the copyright on
bottom-slapping.

In Old English,
the word 'ears' meant 'arse'.

In the 1800s,
ducks were called 'arsefeet'
because their feet are so
close to their bottoms.

People's body temperature
drops when they watch videos
of other people putting their
hands into cold water.

During the Cold War,
the US tested supersonic
ejector seats
on bears.

In Switzerland,
if you fail your driving test
three times, you have to
visit a psychologist
to explain why.

In 1966,
Mercedes introduced a car
steered with a joystick.

The first pram
had a harness so it
could be pulled by a
dog or a goat.

Sloths have
more bones in their necks
than giraffes.

'Derbyshire neck'
was an 18th-century name for
swollen thyroid glands.

'Token-suckers'
are people who steal
New York City metro tokens.

French pubic lice are
known as *papillons d'amour*,
'butterflies of love'.

A Shakespearean euphemism
for infidelity is 'groping for trout
in a peculiar river'.

All of Shakespeare's
six known signatures are
spelt differently and not one is spelt
'William Shakespeare'.

The first recorded use
of 'pop' as in 'pop music'
was in a letter written
by George Eliot
in 1862.

'Lolz', 'shizzle', 'bezzy'
and 'emoji' are all acceptable
Scrabble words.

The song 'Yes, We Have
No Bananas' was written by
Leon Trotsky's nephew.

Bananas emit
antimatter.

Under a black light
bananas glow
blue.

You can't make
blue fireworks.

In ancient China,
archers attached sparklers
to their arrows.

St Peter's School, York,
never celebrates Bonfire Night.
Its most famous old boy
is Guy Fawkes.

Barack Obama's
mother's name was Stanley.
Her nickname at school
was 'Stan the man'.

Buzz Aldrin's father
was friends with
Orville Wright.

Boeing test the
Wi-Fi signal on their planes
by filling the seats with
sacks of potatoes.

The White House
had no Wi-Fi
until 2012.

Thomas Jefferson kept
sheep on the White House lawn.
They were vicious and attacked
anyone who went near them.

Theodore Roosevelt
had a pet hyena.

Napoleon
had a pet wombat.

The Hawaiian pizza
was invented by a Greek
in Canada.

There is an
Indian women's
basketball player called
Elizabeth Hilarious.

Catherine of Aragon
wasn't present at any of her
first three weddings.

Throughout the 19th century,
between a third and a half of
British brides were pregnant
on their wedding day.

A *paraclausithyron*
is a love song performed
outside the beloved's
front door.

'Mambo No. 5' was
the theme song for the
2000 Democratic Convention
until someone noticed the line
'A little bit of Monica in my life'.

Cats enjoy classical music
but are much less interested
in pop music.

When P. L. Travers
went on *Desert Island Discs*,
she didn't pick any music at all
but chose poetry instead.

Despite the line in the song
'Fairytale of New York',
'the boys of the NYPD'
don't have a choir.

The composer of
'Jingle Bells'
also wrote the song
'We Conquer or Die'.

Marching in unison
makes men more
aggressive.

Counting money
makes you feel
less pain.

Counting the rings
in a mammoth's tusks
tells you its age.

When hunting,
humpback whales
make a 'tick tock' sound
that tells other whales
it's dinnertime.

English has more words
for the noises dogs make
than any other language.

Tapping a dashboard
makes a pleasant noise because
motor manufacturers discovered
that one in four people do it
when buying a new car.

In 1999,
Harley-Davidson
tried to trademark the sound
of their engines revving.

People
who can taste sounds
have 'lexical gustatory
synaesthesia'.

Hodor
in *Game of Thrones*
(who can only say his own name)
suffers from 'expressive aphasia'.

Admiral Nelson
suffered from chronic
seasickness.

Every week,
four ships sink
somewhere in the world.

94% of the Earth's oceans
are in permanent
pitch darkness.

In the German resort of Travemünde,
all sandcastles must be knocked
down at the end of each day
so nobody trips over them
in the dark.

It takes about
200 tons of sand to
build one detached
house.

The defence policy of New Zealand's
McGillicuddy Serious Party was
to leave beer on all beaches to
distract any invading army.

William the Conqueror
banned capital punishment;
criminals had their eyes
or testicles removed.

In Saxon England,
selling blood sausages was
punishable by the loss of property,
then being 'severely purged',
'disgracefully shaved'
and exiled.

In 1969,
an Italian man was charged with
selling 'grated Parmesan cheese'
that turned out to be grated
umbrella handles.

In 2014,
a man arrested in Lincoln for
growing 28 cannabis plants
in his garage was called
Mr Hippy.

Children called Joseph, Cameron,
William and Jake are naughtier than
those called Jacob, Daniel,
Thomas and James.

Since *Breaking Bad* started,
four times as many babies in the UK
have been named Walter.

Pippi Longstocking's full name is Pippilotta Delicatessa Windowshade Mackrelmint Ephraim's Daughter Longstocking.

Baristas
in the Starbucks at the
CIA's headquarters don't write
the customers' names
on the cups.

A large latte
contains more saturated fat than
a cream doughnut.

To replace energy after a workout,
most sports supplements
are no more effective
than a burger.

Two tablespoons of dried basil
contain the same amount of calcium
as a glass of milk.

The last thing Charles II ate
before he died was an 'antidote'
containing 'extracts of all the herbs
and animals of the kingdom'.

One in eight
people in the world
go to bed hungry.

The more recently a judge has eaten,
the more likely they are
to grant parole.

The first man to
send a Valentine's card was
a Frenchman imprisoned
in the Tower of London.

Some American jails now dress inmates
in black and white jumpsuits because
the TV show *Orange Is the New Black*
has made the orange ones too cool.

Prisoners in California can
reduce their sentences
by opting to fight
forest fires.

Denmark
imports
prisoners.

The time machine
in *Back to the Future*
was originally going to be a fridge;
it was changed to a car in case
it encouraged children to
climb into fridges.

One working title
for *Toy Story* was
'Toyz in the Hood'.

Robin Williams
improvised so much of *Aladdin*
it became ineligible for the Oscar for
Best Original Screenplay.

Half of the world's
Californian condors were
raised in captivity by
glove puppets.

Jugglers
in medieval Germany
were not allowed to
inherit property.

Until the reign of Henry VIII,
kitchen assistants in the
royal household
worked naked.

Il y a une couille dans le potage
('There is a testicle in the soup')
is French slang for
'There is a major problem.'

The largest lake in
Slovenia disappears
every year.

Ancient Sparta held a
'Festival of the Naked Boys'
every year.

The ancient Romans
collected souvenir mugs.

The Minoans,
not the Romans,
invented the aqueduct.

The Greek for
'It's Greek to me' translates as
'This strikes me as Chinese.'

The Chinese political faction
known as the Gang of Four
had six members.

37 is the 12th prime number
and 73 is the 21st prime number.

2015
is a palindrome in binary:
11111011111

Beethoven
never learnt how to do
multiplication.

J. S. Bach
always carried a dagger to
protect himself from
students.

Sigmund Freud
kept a porcupine on his desk
as a reminder of the 'prickliness'
of human relationships.

Franz Kafka
destroyed 90% of
everything he wrote.

Victor Hugo
found writing so hard
to get down to he asked his valet to
lock up all his clothes and not
give them back till he'd
written something.

Wearing
a Superman T-shirt
significantly boosts your
self-confidence.

Queen Victoria wore
crotchless underwear.

Abraham Lincoln used to hide
important documents in
his stovepipe hat.

James Joyce
always kept a pair of
doll's knickers in
his pocket.

Signs saying
'Beware of Pickpockets'
attract pickpockets.

Male kangaroos
attract females by
showing off their biceps.

Kangaroos
swim doggy-paddle.

Due to flash floods,
one of the biggest dangers
in the desert is
drowning.

Only 30%
of the Sahara desert
is sand.

The word 'scruples'
comes from the Latin *scrupulus*,
a small sharp stone that got
caught in your sandal.

The most painful place
to be stung by a bee is
inside your nostril.

Most honeybees in the US
live in hives stored
on flatbed trucks.

Ants' nests
can get infested by
smaller ants.

Dragonflies can migrate
11,000 miles
a year.

Insects in New York consume
60,000 hot dogs' worth of
discarded junk food
each year.

Morbidly obese people who are
too large for hospital MRI machines
may have to get their scans
done at the zoo.

Most of the fat
lost when dieting is
exhaled as carbon dioxide.

There is more
toxic nitrogen dioxide
in London's Oxford Street
than anywhere else
in the world.

In the 14th century,
London had a higher murder rate
than any US city today.

A London by-law of 1351
prohibited boys from playing
practical jokes on MPs.

In the 19th century,
many main roads into London
were paved with wood.

If a woodchuck could
chuck wood, it would chuck
700 lb of wood per day.

'Limericks'
were originally ladies' gloves
made from chicken skin
or calves' foetuses.

Baby parking
is Italian for
crèche.

Only 3% of children of
atheist parents go on to join
a religious faith, compared to 50%
if both parents are religious.

To treat his childhood asthma,
Theodore Roosevelt's doctor and
parents encouraged him
to smoke cigars.

In the 2001 general election, the
Official Monster Raving Loony Party
promised to reduce class sizes by
'making the children stand
closer together'.

In the 2005 general election,
one candidate stood in 13
different constituencies.

In 19th-century US elections,
you had to cut your own
ballot paper out of
the newspaper.

The first newspaper
in English was printed
in Amsterdam.

London's first
telephone directory
didn't have any
numbers in it.

The first known genitals
belonged to jawed vertebrates
called *Microbrachius dicki.*

There are
328 people in the US
called Abcde.

Napoleon let
the sons of the fallen
in his army add the name
Napoleon to their own.

During his campaign in Egypt,
Napoleon sent the locals
64,000 pints of wine –
but only after it
had gone off.

At a food-safety conference
in Baltimore in 2014,
100 attendees got
food poisoning.

After feeding near
an M&M's factory in 2012,
French bees started producing
blue and green honey.

The giant green sea anemone
eats seabird chicks that fall
from nearby cliffs.

Most adult cats
are lactose intolerant.

Wimbledon keeps its
tennis balls
at a temperature of
exactly 20°C.

The best time of the day
for hand–eye co-ordination
is 8 p.m.

On New Year's Eve 2014,
835 of the 1,000 police officers
meant to be on duty in Rome
phoned in sick.

US presidents Washington, Lincoln,
Monroe, Jackson, Grant, Garfield,
Theodore Roosevelt and Kennedy
all suffered from malaria.

A *cyberchondriac* is someone who
scours the Internet looking for
details of their illnesses.

The computer system
of Britain's police force is called the
Home Office Large Major Enquiry System:
HOLMES for short.

A fifth of the candidates
in India's 2014 general election
faced criminal charges.

The Yakuza crime syndicate of Japan
has launched a website and theme tune
to attract new members.

Butch Cassidy's first crime was
stealing a pair of jeans and a pie.
He left an IOU, but the shopkeeper
reported him anyway.

By law, all buses in
Argentina must carry the words
Las Malvinas son Argentinas:
'The Falklands are
Argentine.'

The first London buses
were so slow that operators
provided free reading matter.

The first mobile library
was horse-drawn.

The most-borrowed book from the
Bank of England's information centre
is an A-level Economics textbook.

The keys used to open
the Bank of England's gold vault
are three feet long.

The world's deepest gold mine is
nearly three miles deep and could hold
ten Empire State Buildings stacked
on top of one another.

The richest person in Asia
is Mr Ka-shing.

When Stephen Hawking gave a lecture
in Japan, he was asked not to mention
the possible re-collapse of the
universe in case it affected
the stock market.

No one knows
who invented
Bitcoin.

Four of the six
founders of PayPal
built bombs at
school.

The surface area
of the world of *Minecraft* is
9,258,235 times larger
than that of Earth.

The opposite of
extraterrestrial is intraterrestrial:
life deep inside the earth.

Eric Cantona
was raised in a cave.

You are three times
more likely to be bitten
by Luis Suárez if you play
football against him than you
are to be bitten by a snake
in a year of living in
Australia.

California
ground squirrels
kick sand into
snakes' faces.

The face of
the average man has
30,000 whiskers.

Roald Dahl
suffered from pogonophobia,
an extreme hatred
of beards.

Gillette's five-bladed razor
was a joke on the website *The Onion*
a year before they got round to
producing a real one.

The first-ever
mobile-phone network
could handle a maximum of
three calls at the same time
in any given city.

The first-ever
YouTube video was
an 18-second clip called
'Me at the Zoo'.

The single biggest expense in
the *LEGO Universe* video game was
hiring a team of moderators to
detect if anyone had built
Lego penises.

The Colorado Rapids
Major League Soccer team play
their home games at 'The Dick'.

The first football match
in Brazil had just 15 spectators:
four family and friends and
eleven tennis players who
were there by accident.

When Uruguay won
the first World Cup in 1930,
it wasn't deemed important enough
for it to be reported in *The Times*.

BBC radio newsreaders
in the 1920s always wore
dinner jackets, even though
no one could see them.

The first BBC radio presenter
with a northern accent was hired in
the Second World War to make it harder
for the Germans to produce
fake news bulletins.

If Scotland left the union,
average annual rainfall in the UK
would decrease by 8 inches.

Between 1901 and 1960,
there was a *coup d'état* in every
independent country on Earth
except Sweden, Switzerland,
Britain and the US.

In 1928,
Liberia's 15,000 registered voters
elected Charles King president
with a majority
of 60,000.

In 1835,
US President Andrew Jackson
beat off a would-be assassin
with his cane.

Wherever he goes,
the US president has his food cooked
by White House stewards to
ensure it is safe to eat.

George Osborne
keeps a padlock on
his office fridge.

Winston Churchill
enshrined the tea break
into law.

Churchill,
Admiral and Sheila's Wheels
are three meerkats who live at
St Andrews Aquarium.

A group of otters
is called a romp.

A group of hyenas
is called a cackle.

To deter foxes,
the actor David Tennant
urinates in his
back garden.

In the Middle Ages,
Scottish warriors used horse urine
to dye their tunics yellow.

King Harold didn't die
at the battle of Hastings
from an arrow in his eye:
he was hacked apart by
four Norman knights.

At the battle of Dybbøl in 1864,
the Prussian assault on the Danes
was accompanied by a 300-man
military orchestra playing a
specially composed march.

There were more Scots
in the army that defeated
Bonnie Prince Charlie at Culloden
than there were in his own army.

Rawgabbit
is Scots for one
who speaks confidently
on a subject about which they
know absolutely nothing.

One job application
for an air traffic controller
in the Scilly Isles
was in Braille.

It takes three million presses
to wear out a button on
an Xbox controller.

The button was invented
more than 1,000 years before
the buttonhole.

John Cage's
composition
'Organ2/ASLSP'
takes 639 years
to play.

Orang-utans
like playing on iPads,
but gorillas don't.

When the iPod Shuffle
was released, it came with
a warning saying,
'Do not eat.'

Apple Inc.
was founded on
April Fool's Day.

April in England,
despite its reputation,
is usually the month with
the lowest rainfall.

In April and May,
sparrows' testicles increase
a thousandfold in size.

Hippos can retract their testicles
over a foot into their body
to stop rivals from
biting them.

The longer a
narwhal's tusk,
the bigger his
testicles.

Queen Victoria
owned two
tricycles.

The first woman
to cycle round the world
learnt to ride a bike
the day before
she set off.

The first riders of
the first loop-the-loop
roller coaster in Paris
were monkeys.

When the waltz
first arrived in London,
it was called an 'obscene display'
best confined to 'prostitutes
and adulteresses'
by *The Times.*

At times
of peak fertility,
women's voices are
higher pitched.

Sleep-deprived
fruit flies take longer
to learn things.

Your brain cells shrink
when you're asleep.

The first person
to study sleepwalking was
Lord Byron's friend John Polidori.
His recommended cures were beatings
and the application of electricity.

Queen Elizabeth I
was wrapped in a red blanket
to cure her smallpox.

King George IV
had eight boxing champions
as his pages for his
coronation.

King Richard II's chefs
wrote a cookbook that
included a recipe for
porpoise porridge.

The Royal Mint
is a cashless workplace.

The first pair of Nike
trainers was made
in a waffle iron.

Kim Jong-un's wife
was a member of North Korea's
national cheerleading squad.

Robert Mugabe's wife Grace
received her PhD from the
University of Zimbabwe
two months after
she enrolled.

Samuel Pepys bought his wife
moisturiser made from
puppies' urine.

Red lipstick
boosts waitresses' tips
from male customers, but not
from female ones.

Cheiloscopy
is the study of lip-prints;
they are as useful to police
as fingerprints.

The fingernails of
the middle fingers grow
faster than the others.

The toenails of
male terrapins are used to
hold onto females
during sex.

When a list of
all-time basketball greats
was assembled in 1940,
the average height
was 5'10".

By the end of her life,
Queen Victoria's bust measured
seven inches more than
her height.

Fear of heights
only begins six weeks after
a baby learns to crawl.

Maternal stress
causes more adverse effects
in male foetuses than
in female ones.

The first home pregnancy test
in the US included a vial
of sheep's blood.

Online sales
of baby equipment
peak at 4 a.m.

80% of dreams
are about normal things
like washing up or
being at work.

5.2% of men have
kissed a monster in their dreams,
3.4% have had foreplay with an animal
and 1.7% have had sex with
an 'object, plant or rock'.

Dreams happening
later in the night are
usually more positive
than earlier ones.

The Chinese
don't 'sleep like a log',
they 'sleep like a
dead pig'.

The man who discovered
rapid eye movement
nearly called it
'jerky eye movement'.

Magic tricks
used to be called
'Hanky Panky'.

Charioteers in ancient Rome
were not allowed to hamper
their opponents with
magic spells.

Early depictions of Jesus
show him with a
magic wand.

*'Kerosene lamp
bilong Jesus gone bugger-up'*
is the expression used by the
Koorie people of New South Wales
to describe solar eclipses.

In the Senegalese version of Firefox,
a 'crash' is a *hookii*, which means
'a cow falling over but
not dying'.

The French
for 1960s pop music
is *yé yé*.

The French
for 'pie chart' is
un camembert.

Until the 1920s,
Camembert
was green.

In 16th-century Venice,
it was the height of fashion
for ladies to colour
their nipples.

Ladyboy gangs in Thailand
apply sedatives to their nipples,
knocking out unsuspecting men who
suck them and can then be robbed
while they're asleep.

Charlie Chaplin
had sex with more than
2,000 women.

Male hedge sparrows
have sex 100 times a day,
but each time takes only
a tenth of a second.

Male honeybees die after sex;
their genitals detach from
their body with
an audible
'pop'.

US slang terms for
sex in the 19th century
included 'fandango de pokum',
'buttock-stirring' and 'being
amongst the parsley'.

400 million years ago,
mushrooms grew
24 feet tall.

An 11-ton mushroom
found in Crystal Falls, Michigan,
was the inspiration for the annual
Humungus Fungus Festival.

Names for British fungi include
the jelly ear, the bearded tooth,
the weeping toothcrust,
the slimy earthtongue,
the foetid parachute and
the hairy nuts disco.

The inky cap mushroom
is edible, but poisonous
if mixed with
alcohol.

Corona beer
is never drunk with
a slice of lime
in Mexico.

There is
an Irish pub
in Guantanamo Bay.

Cuban
emergency services
use sniffer
rabbits.

KitKats
in sweet-potato
flavour are available
in Japan.

Sweden has
a ski-through
McDonald's.

The US is
visited by more
missionaries than
any other country.

Medical students
in 18th-century Scotland
could pay their tuition fees
in corpses.

In 18th-century England,
'delivering a flying pasty'
was wrapping poo in paper
and throwing it over a
neighbour's wall.

Modern sewage systems use
more than 1,000 tons of water to
move each ton of solid waste.

It takes 100 times as much water
to make Coke cans and bottles
as it does to make the
Coca-Cola itself.

10% of all the water
in ancient Rome went
to the emperor.

The Roman emperor Commodus
renamed every month of the year
after himself and rechristened
Rome 'Commodiana'.

The Roman Empire
was only the 17th biggest
empire in history.

Types of Roman gladiator included
essedarii, who rode chariots,
laquearii, who had lassos,
and *andabata*, who
fought blindfold.

In flight,
bats' hearts beat
1,000 times a minute.

Before they can take off,
bees have to warm up their
flight muscles.

Early aerobatic display teams
tied their biplanes together
before taking off.

'To take off
your considering cap'
was an 18th-century
euphemism for
being drunk.

The logo for the
Royal New Zealand Air Force
is the (flightless) kiwi.

The man who
invented and flew
the first airship held rehearsal
dinner parties with 10-foot-high
tables and chairs to simulate
dining in mid-air.

Doritos
were invented at
Disneyland.

The sports bra
was invented in the 1970s
by sewing two jockstraps
together.

Bill Lear invented both
the Lear Jet and the
8-track cartridge.

The selfie stick
was invented
in the 1920s.

E-cigarettes
were invented
in 1963.

The Inuit word
tawakiqutiqarpiit
means 'do you have
any tobacco for sale?'

Ottoman emperor
Murad the Cruel put
25,000 people to death
for smoking.

The punishment for smoking
in 17th-century Russia
was castration.

Castration prevents
male-pattern baldness,
providing it is done before
any hair is lost.

The male-pattern baldness
of King Louis XIII meant French
aristocrats wore wigs
for 200 years.

For 200 years
after tomatoes reached Europe,
they were grown for purely
ornamental reasons.

Red tomatoes evolved
as a result of a meteorite strike
60 million years ago.

Eating a British-grown tomato
is three times as bad for the
environment as eating
one grown in Spain.

Spain has
more vineyards
than France.

Oklahoma has
more earthquakes
than California.

On 28 August 2014,
1,187 earthquakes were
recorded in Iceland –
almost one a minute.

Every public tweet
is recorded in the
Library of Congress.

Going to the library
produces as much happiness
as a £1,359 pay rise.
Going to the gym
is like losing
£1,318.

In the 18th century,
'to vowel' was to issue
an IOU after losing
at gambling.

Dostoevsky
wrote *The Gambler* to
pay off his gambling debts.

The 1950 book
How to Survive an Atomic Bomb
recommended wearing a hat
to shield you from
the atomic flash.

'Bang novel' is
the literal translation
of the Danish for
'thriller'.

Napoleon wrote a
romantic novella aged 27,
when he was already a
successful general.

Before he wrote *Tarzan*,
Edgar Rice Burroughs was
a pencil-sharpener salesman.

Roald Dahl was
buried with a bottle of Burgundy,
his snooker cues, a power saw
and some chocolate.

Bela Lugosi was
buried in the cape he wore
in the movie *Dracula*.

Leonard Nimoy's
two autobiographies are called
I Am Not Spock and
I Am Spock.

Dolly Parton
has a theme park
called Dollywood.

Mazes in Germany
are called *Irrgarten,*
or 'error gardens'.

Sheep in mazes
tend to turn left.

A volunteer shepherd
is called a 'lookerer'.

Camel spiders move
so fast they are called
'Kalahari Ferraris'.

Boudoir
is French for
'pouting room'.

Danish law
makes it illegal to
desecrate the flags of
foreign countries but
legal to burn the
Danish flag.

The Russian flag is
planted at the North Pole,
at the bottom of the Arctic Ocean.

Floating in the world's oceans
are 5.25 trillion pieces
of plastic.

The silverware
on the *Titanic* included
100 pairs of grape scissors,
1,000 oyster forks and
2,000 egg spoons.

The champagne
in a 170-year-old bottle
found on the Baltic seabed was
described by wine experts as
'sometimes cheesy' with
'elements of wet hair'.

In France a
'champagne socialist'
is a 'caviar lefty'.

In France a
'can of worms'
is a 'basket of crabs'.

The last public guillotining
in France took place in 1939.
The actor Christopher Lee
was there to see it.

A pig was hanged for
sacrilege in France
in 1394 for eating
a communion
wafer.

9 out of 10
onions are eaten in
the country they
were grown in.

Portugal is the
only country in the world
where all drugs
are legal.

Saudi Arabia is the
only country in the world
with no national women's
football team.

The only countries
in the world that don't have
paternity leave as standard
are Papua New Guinea
and the US.

Less than 1% of
the shoes sold in America
were made there.

Since 1970,
the average female shoe size
has increased from
a four to a six.

Nike owns
a patent on
self-lacing trainers.

Prince Charles's valet
irons his shoelaces.

Prince Albert
commissioned a
corrugated-iron ballroom
for Balmoral Castle.

The first credit card
was made of cardboard.

Replacement eyelids
can be made from
foreskins.

Noël Coward's way
to make a perfect martini was
to fill a glass with gin and wave it
in the general direction
of Italy.

60% of the alcohol
in America is drunk by
10% of the people.

In the 18th century,
Harvard University had
three breweries
on campus.

A sperm cell
takes twice as long to mature
as Heineken lager.

Human cells contain
all the necessary genes
to make feathers.

Birds practise their songs
quietly in private before they
perform them in public.

Baby elephants
have milk tusks.

Baby turtles
call to each other while
they're still in their shells
so that they all hatch
at the same time.

The shell of
an armadillo is
so tough that bullets
bounce off it.

The largest military tank
was made by Porsche
for the Nazis.

For six weeks in 1941,
the crew of HMS *Trident* shared
their submarine with a reindeer
called Pollyanna.

After the Falklands War,
the Argentinian surrender document
was mislaid by the British
for over a year.

Until the 1990s,
Britain's nuclear weapons were
secured with bike locks.

Britons are
16 times more likely to
understand the rules of Quidditch
than the rules of croquet.

The House of Lords is the
second-biggest legislative chamber
in the world after the Chinese
National People's Congress.

The national anthem
of Ukraine is called
'Ukraine Is Not Dead Yet'.

You cannot kill a sponge
with your bare hands.

The hydraulic tools
used by rescue workers to extract
people trapped under heavy objects
are called the Jaws of Life.

The word 'cemetery'
is from the ancient Greek
for dormitory.

The Latin for pizza is
placenta compressa, or
'compressed cake'.

The Museum of Bread Culture
in Ulm, Germany, has a collection
of over 18,000 objects,
none of which is bread.

The Nazis celebrated Christmas
with chocolate SS men and
swastika-shaped tree lights.

Mussolini
was once employed by
MI5.

Abraham Lincoln
was 6'4" tall and wore
a seven-inch hat.

President Grover Cleveland
used to urinate out of the
window of the Oval Office.

Johnny Cash
was the first American
to hear that Stalin had died.
He was an air force
radio operator.

To identify
each other in the dark,
soldiers in both world wars
put bioluminescent fungi
on their helmets.

The silent documentary
The Battle of the Somme (1916) sold
more tickets in British cinemas
than *Star Wars*.

An early title
for *Star Wars* was
'Adventures of the Starkiller'.

Movie trailers
are so named because
they used to come after,
or 'trail', the movie.

The trailer for
the longest-ever movie is
72 minutes long.

In 2014,
the longest-serving
Girl Guide in the UK
turned 106.

There are more Boy Scouts
in Indonesia than in the
rest of the world
combined.

The word
'hundred'
used to mean
120.

The Turkish
for 'breakfast'
translates as
'before coffee'.

There are 125
species of coffee plant
but we only make coffee
from six of them.

More than half
the world's mountains have
not yet been climbed.

In 2006,
volunteers removing
litter from Ben Nevis found
a piano near the summit.

Almost one in five
Beatles songs mention
the weather.

On 24 March 2015,
the temperature in Antarctica was
higher than in Madrid, Malta
and Marrakesh.

A third of the people
living in Monaco are
millionaires.

The most money you can fit
in a standard-sized briefcase
is $780,000.

19% of Americans
think they're in the
top 1% of earners.

Men think they are
much better at maths
than they really are.

Women are
more efficient than men at
gathering mushrooms.

In the first edition of
the *Encyclopaedia Britannica*,
the entry for 'woman' read
'the female of man'.

Action Man's
actual name is
Matthew Exler.

Graham Greene
once entered a competition
to parody his own writing style.
He came second.

A nanosecond
is to a second what
a second is to
32 years.

At one per second,
counting all the brain's
synapses would take
three million years.

For 50 million years,
birds had snouts,
not beaks.

Dinosaurs
communicated
by hissing.

Female buffaloes
make decisions
by voting.

John Wayne
loved wearing his Stetson
so much he had the roof
of his car raised.

Levi's jeans
were originally called
'waist overalls'.

The first beach huts
were called
'bathing bungalows'.

If Bilbo Baggins's Hobbit hole
were for sale in southern England,
it would be on the market
at £8.5 million.

If Tuvalu sold its
embassy building in Wimbledon,
it could pay off more than a
tenth of its national debt.

More than half of the world's
cash transactions are carried out
to hide something from
the authorities.

People are more likely to lie
in the afternoon than
in the morning.

The answer to a
True or False question
is most likely
to be true.

45% of people
falsely claim to have
been skydiving.

One in 20 people
have hallucinated
at some point
in their life.

95% of people
are immune to
leprosy.

One treatment
for strychnine poisoning
in the 19th century was
to drink melted lard.

The microbes
living in your stomach
suffer from jet lag.

More insects
are killed by cars in
the UK each year than
human beings have
ever lived.

Toyota sold
18.7 million cars
from 2012 to 2014,
but had to recall
20 million.

Vespas are
banned from
the centre of
Rome.

In ancient Rome,
bakers were forbidden
from mixing with
comedians.

Competitors in the
Hong Kong ultramarathon
run up and down the same
stretch of road 25 times.

The 1863 Derby
had 32 false starts,
delaying the start of the race
by over an hour.

The world record for
horse long jump is shorter
than the world record for
human long jump.

The longest word
with all its letters in
reverse alphabetical order
is 'spoonfeed'.

The Bodleian Library in Oxford
got its first Chinese book in 1604.
It was 80 years before they
found someone who
could read it.

To read all the books
in the British Library at
a rate of five a day would
take 80,000 years.

The autobiography
of Colonel Sanders was called
*Life as I Know It Has Been
Finger Lickin' Good.*

The man who
first had the idea of
using microwaves to cook food
got a one-off payment of $2.

The first published version
of 'Old Mother Hubbard'
was dedicated to a
Mr Bastard.

The first monorail
was horse-drawn.

The first powered submarine
was called the *Resurgam*, meaning
'I will rise again', but it sank
almost immediately.

The first version of *Hamlet*
was called 'Amleth' and has
a happy ending.

Judi Dench
first appeared on
stage at the age of five.
She played a snail.

Children grow
faster in spring.

Spring gets shorter
by about 30 seconds
every year.

Flowers
get suntans.

Ants yawn
and stretch their legs
when they wake up.

Spiders evolved
100 million years
before flies.

Ten midges
make a swarm.

More than a quarter
of the world's population
regularly eat insects.

A recent scientific study
has concluded that there are
too many scientific studies.

182 billion emails
are sent every day,
26 for every person
on the planet.

In the 1870s,
North America had
144 official time zones.

In the time it takes to say
'one hundred and thirty',
your vocal cords
open and close
130 times.

When you're talking
to someone face-to-face,
your pupils dilate to
match theirs.

The word 'huh'
is understood in all
known languages.

The word 'twerk'
has been in use
since 1820.

Until AD 837,
Halloween was on
12 May.

Pancake Day was
celebrated in the 17th century by
'cock-throwing' – beating a chicken
to death with cudgels.

Until 1970,
all pubs in Ireland
closed on St Patrick's Day.

88%
of New Year's
resolutions
fail.

Poecilonym
is a synonym
for the word
'synonym'.

Lachschlaganfall is
the condition where
a person laughs so much
they fall unconscious.

In Old English,
the word 'thing'
meant 'a parliament'.

The word 'aficionado'
originally meant 'a
bullfighting fan'.

Cow bells
make cows feel
stressed.

The pouches
in hamsters' cheeks
go all the way back
to their hips.

Bats
get erections
in their tongues.

Snails
use mucus to
seal their shells with
a transparent 'door'.

Scientists
have discovered
a species of algae that
tastes like bacon.

The portable machine gun was
invented by Hiram Maxim,
who also invented the
mousetrap.

In Toronto in 2008,
mice chewed through wires in
the ceiling of an animal shelter
and killed nearly 100 cats.

In 1901,
Edith Wagner
of New York married
her Maltese cat.

Cerberus,
the name of the
three-headed dog
that guarded Hell,
is Sanskrit for
'Spot'.

Dog food
is tested on
humans.

Wild boars
wash their food.

A Siberian tit can
store half a million seeds
in a single winter.

In severe solar storms,
Earth loses 100 tons of its
atmosphere into space.

The dialling code for space
is the same as the
one for Texas.

The number of
American teenagers who
consider themselves 'very important'
increased from 12% in 1950
to 80% in 2010.

Twice as many
American schoolgirls
would rather be a celebrity's PA
than president of Harvard.

The Harvard–Yale
boat race takes place
on a river called
the Thames.

London, Ontario,
is on a river called
the Thames.

When Columbus
travelled to America,
he thought he was
sailing uphill.

The first bus in Britain
to be powered by human excrement
ran from Bristol to Bath on
the Number 2 route.

There is a river
in Nicaragua called
the Pis-Pis.

There are 10,685 beaches
in Australia.

People from
South Sudan, Palestine,
São Tomé and Príncipe, Myanmar
or the Solomon Islands can travel
visa-free to 28 countries.
UK citizens can
visit 147.

'MEXICO CITY'
was a postal acronym in
the Second World War meaning
'May Every Kiss [X] I Can Offer
Carry Itself to You'.

The number 88
is Morse code shorthand for
'love and kisses'.

Morse code
was expanded in 2004 to include
._ _._. meaning '@'.

Makahakahaka
is Hawaiian for
'deep-set eyeballs'.

No words in
Esperanto are more than
12 letters long.

In Norway,
to change your surname to
one that fewer than 200 people have
you must ask permission from
everyone who has that name.

In Finland,
reindeers' antlers are covered with
reflective paint so drivers
can see them.

Åland is the
only region of Finland to
have a single official language.
It's Swedish.

Swiss cheese
is losing its holes.

Jamaica, Colombia and Saint Lucia
are the only countries in the world
where your boss is more likely
to be a woman than a man.

Three times more men than women
would pretend not to notice
if a friend broke
down in tears.

Until 1964,
women in France
needed their husbands' permission to
start a business, get a passport
or open a bank account.

The revolving door was invented
by a man who hated holding
doors open for women.

Twister was described
as 'sex in a box' by
rival manufacturers who
tried to have it banned.

The meagre fish
is so noisy during sex that
it gives away its location
to fishermen, who can
then catch it.

When *National Geographic*
published its first wildlife photos
in 1906, two board members
resigned in disgust.

All worm sex
takes place in
the '69' position.

The Bassian thrush
farts when feeding;
this startles worms into
revealing their location.

Pigeons
don't bob their heads if
they are walking on
a treadmill.

To prepare for
China's national day,
10,000 ceremonial pigeons have
anal security checks.

In March 2014,
an Australian python
swallowed a chihuahua and
found itself chained to a kennel.

Ernest Hemingway
hunted sharks with
a machine gun.

Nikola Tesla
hated pearls so much that he
refused to speak to women
who wore them.

Samantha Cameron was
taught to play pool at university
by rap star Tricky.

Alex Salmond
changed his signature after
the Queen told him off for his
messy handwriting.

Martin Luther King Jr
got a C+ in Public
Speaking.

Bill Clinton
learnt jujitsu before
meeting Yasser Arafat
in case he tried
to hug him.

Barbra Streisand
had a shopping mall
built for her exclusive use
underneath her house.

While playing
Achilles in the movie *Troy*,
Brad Pitt injured his
Achilles tendon.

Jackie, the second
Metro-Goldwyn-Mayer lion,
survived two train wrecks, an earthquake,
a boat sinking, a studio explosion and a
plane crash in the Arizona desert.

For each lion cub that survives,
a lioness will have mated
3,000 times.

85% of male insects
engage in homosexual activity,
but often by mistake.

To flirt,
haddocks
hum.

Only 28% of people
know when they're
being flirted with.

The 'Mile High Club' is defined
by the *Oxford English Dictionary* as
'an imaginary association of people'.

There is a consultant urologist
at Musgrove Park hospital in
Taunton, Somerset, called
Nicholas Burns-Cox.

In hot weather,
the Eiffel Tower grows
by six inches.

Almost all kangaroos
are left-handed.

The first animals
with fingers had
seven or eight
on each hand.

Charles Darwin thought
the menstrual cycle was evidence that
early humans lived by the sea and
synchronised their lives
with the tides.

9 out of 10 chimps
look both ways when
crossing the road.

The DVLA has banned
the number plate VA61ANA,
but has allowed PEN15.

Until the 1960s,
women were banned from
wearing trousers in the
Houses of Parliament.

Women in 18th-century England
who remarried but didn't want to carry
their debts over to the new marriage
had to get married in the nude.

The US nude-wedding industry
is worth $440 million a year.

There are nearly
twice as many calories
in human blood
as in beer.

Ancient Sumerian beer
was as thick as porridge and was
drunk through a straw.

To shave two seconds
off the time it takes you to
eat a pie in a pie-eating competition,
drink cough syrup beforehand.

In 2015,
the president of Belarus
officially stated that
'Belarusian sausage does not
contain toilet paper.'

In the 18th century,
King George I declared
all pigeon droppings to be
property of the Crown.

The Duke of Edinburgh's
pet names for the Queen include
'cabbage' and 'sausage'.

The world record
for the most sausages
produced in one minute
is 36.

More than
150 billion animals
are killed by humans
every year.

The number of hospital deaths
investigated by autopsy has
fallen from 40% in 1960
to less than 1% today.

Sumo wrestling referees
traditionally carry a knife
so if they make a bad decision
they can kill themselves.

Professional boxing
is banned in Cuba because
the prize money is incompatible
with Marxism.

Pigeon breeding
and skinny jeans are both
banned by ISIS.

In 2013,
46 girls born in the UK
were named Isis.

Barbie and Ken
are named after the
daughter and son of the
couple who invented them.

There are more than
2,000 Americans
named Santa.

All the 126
remaining kakapos
have names.

Pelé's
first name is Edson:
he was named after
Thomas Edison.

Three-quarters of all the
boys christened in England in the
mid-13th century were named
John, Thomas, Robert,
Richard or William.

Uranus was
originally called
George.

The surnames
of Bradley Cooper
and Michael Fassbender both
mean 'barrel-maker'.

Stephen King's son
is called Joe King.

Grumpy Cat
earns more than
Gwyneth Paltrow.

Mark Zuckerberg,
Carlos Slim and Bill Gates are
each worth more in billions of dollars
than their age in years.

When John Lennon appeared on
The Old Grey Whistle Test
in 1975, he was paid in
chocolate biscuits.

Hawaii consumes
more Spam than the 49 other
US states combined.

In 29 US states,
it is still legal to fire someone
for being gay.

In 1960,
Denys Tucker was fired from
his job at the Natural History Museum
because he claimed to have seen
the Loch Ness Monster.

A Tyrannosaurus rex
could outrun
Mo Farah.

When Usain Bolt ran the 100m
at the 2012 London Olympics,
his feet only touched the ground
for two seconds.

Pro snooker player Bill Werbeniuk
could only play when drunk,
so was able to offset the
cost of beer against
his income tax.

Glasgow City Council
spends £10,000 every year
removing traffic cones from
the head of a statue of the
Duke of Wellington.

State senators in Minnesota
are not allowed to make eye contact
with each other during debates.

In 2014,
Italian parliamentary barbers
had their annual salary cut from
£106,000 to £77,000 as an
austerity measure.

In 2013,
a construction company
collecting rubble to repair a road
destroyed a Mayan
pyramid.

In 1963,
George Harrison wrote
to Beatles fans asking them to
stop throwing sweets at him
during concerts.

In 1953,
a new reservoir in New York
flooded the town of
Neversink.

The first flashing lights
on Broadway had an attendant
sitting on a nearby roof to
switch them on and off.

In the early days of baseball,
umpires sat behind
the home plate in
rocking chairs.

Until the late 19th century,
the age of consent in
most US states was
10 years old.

Most of the 'carving'
at Mount Rushmore was
done with dynamite.

There are more pieces
of the Berlin Wall spread
around the world than
there are left in Berlin.

For 1.4 million years
there was no improvement in
the design of stone hand axes.

The ladders of the
San Francisco fire department
are made of wood.

There's as much iron
in 16 pints of Guinness
as there is in one pint
of orange juice.

Feeding oregano
to cows reduces their
methane emissions
by almost half.

Excited guinea pigs
perform little hops
and leaps called
'popcorning'.

Airymouse
is Cornish
for 'bat'.

A mouse's body
grows six new hairs
for each one plucked out.

A whale's nerves are
three times more elastic
than a human's.

Sloth sex
takes under
two minutes.

Most ducks
don't quack.

Owls are
70 times less likely
to hoot when
it's raining.

The Earth's atmosphere
contains more than
15 trillion tons
of water.

Dissolving
Viagra in water
stops flowers wilting
for up to a week.

Sweat
contains
antibiotics.

The word
'nuppence'
means 'no money'.

Poker player
Archie Karas turned
$50 into $40 million
between 1992 and 1994, and
lost it all in 1995.

Americans put out
$3 billion worth of food
for birds every year.

Drunk birds
slur their songs.

Swifts can sleep
on the wing.

Lisa
is Russian
for 'fox'.

The president
of Sinn Féin unwinds
by trampolining
naked with
his dog.

Professional
dog walkers earn
more than
nurses.

The scrotum water frog
of Lake Titicaca is on the verge
of extinction due to its use
as an aphrodisiac.

On Vanuatu,
the native pigs develop
both male and female sex organs
and are used as currency.

A group of chimps in Zambia
wear a blade of grass
in their left ear as a
fashion statement.

It's illegal in
New York City
to take a selfie
with a tiger.

Q

Polar bears
eat dolphins and
freeze the leftovers.

Orang-utans
breastfeed their young
for eight years.

Each of an octopus's
1,600 suckers has 10,000
taste receptors.

In 2014,
scientists named
18,000 new species.

In ancient Greece,
evidence from slaves was
only accepted in court if it was
obtained by torture.

53 of the 84 warrants issued
for torture in British history were
authorised by Queen Elizabeth I.

In the reign of Queen Mary,
anyone caught living idly
for three days was
branded with
'V' for vagrant.

The Thuggees,
a 19th-century Indian gang,
killed at least a million people.
Their favourite weapon was
a handkerchief.

When the Roman emperor
Heraclius entered battle,
his soldiers would applaud to
intimidate their enemies.

Ancient Chinese warriors
showed off by
juggling before battle.

During the First World War,
women giving out white feathers to
'cowards' often did so by mistake
to soldiers who weren't in uniform.

More than a quarter
of new cars in the UK
are white.

Children on long car journeys
are more likely to grow up to be
rich and successful if they
sit in the middle seat.

The Mr Men were
created by Roger Hargreaves
after his son asked what
a tickle looked like.

In the 1960s,
Italian shops had a service
called 'the Smearing' in which they would
spread Nutella on any slice of bread
brought to them by a child.

'Ebb' and 'Flow'
are two NASA satellites.

3D printing means
that NASA can email
tools into space.

Tom Cruise
helped design
NASA's website.

James Cameron
sold his *Terminator* script
for $1.

In the 19th century,
you could be committed to an asylum
for 'novel-reading'.

In 1939,
novelist John Buchan
signed the declaration of war
between Germany
and Canada.

Franz Kafka
convinced his family that
Einstein's theory of relativity
would cure his TB.

People with haemorrhoids
are more than twice as likely
to read on the loo as
those who don't.

The smell of your farts
is as unique as your
fingerprints.

Eunuchs
live 15 years longer than
the average man.

The poke-me-boy tree
only grows on the
Virgin Islands.

One in 10 Britons
describe themselves
as 'very good lovers'.

A third of married Britons
describe sex as
'a chore'.

Almost half of ASDA customers
study other shoppers' baskets
to try to work out if
they are single.

After meeting their mistresses,
ancient Egyptian husbands
chewed garlic to hide any
incriminating odours.

Smelling
a happy person's sweat can
make you happier.

Testosterone
evolved from
oestrogen.

In the 16th century,
women in labour were given
'groaning' beer to drink during
and after the birth.

The Isle of Rhum
used to be called the Isle of Rum.
The 'h' was added by
teetotal Victorians.

The Museum of London has
a whole drawer of codpieces that
one embarrassed Victorian curator
catalogued as 'shoulder pads'.

The average bra
can support the weight
of three bricks.

Paper money in
ancient China bore the inscription
'All Counterfeiters Will
Be Decapitated'.

Counterfeiters
in medieval Russia were
punished by having their coins melted
and the molten metal poured
down their throats.

During the financial crisis of 1720,
Parliament debated a resolution that
bankers be sewn into sacks filled with
poisonous snakes and thrown
into the Thames.

All swimmers
leave traces of faecal matter
in the water.

Two people die,
somewhere on Earth,
every second.

Half of your friends
are replaced every
seven years.

A group of friends in
Washington state have
been playing a game of tag
for more than 24 years.

The largest-ever
game of musical chairs had
8,238 participants.

If you unravelled
every Slinky ever sold,
the wire would circle the Earth
more than 171 times.

The Earth's magnetic field
is 100 times weaker than
a fridge magnet.

Smaller magnets mean
children are swallowing
five times as many as
they did ten years ago.

It is impossible
to hum and whistle
at the same time.

Categories at the
Good Funeral Awards include
Cemetery of the Year, Embalmer
of the Year and Gravedigger
of the Year.

Oxford University's
Future of Humanity Institute
puts the chances of humans
becoming extinct by 2100
at 19%.

After President Eisenhower had
a heart attack, his doctor prescribed
a course of hugs with his wife Mamie.

The Celts thought that
shooting pains in the body were
caused by being shot with
an arrow by an elf.

The most popular song
played at funerals in the UK
is Monty Python's 'Always Look on
the Bright Side of Life'.

On the day he died,
Martin Luther King Jr
had a pillow fight.

A third of
British adults sleep
with a cuddly toy.

A recent poll has found that
if you want someone to fancy you,
QI is the TV programme
you should claim
to watch.

Don't Believe a Word of It?

*Facts are ventriloquists' dummies. Sitting
on a wise man's knee they may be made
to utter words of wisdom; elsewhere, they
say nothing, or talk nonsense.*

ALDOUS HUXLEY

For anyone wishing to verify any of the
facts in the book, this can be done online
by going to qi.com/1234 and typing the
relevant hardcover page number into the
search box. Click on the online sources for a
wide range of background material. Please
do let us know if you have a quibble or a
correction, and add your own discoveries
via our Twitter account @qikipedia.

Acknowledgements

None of this would have been possible without the doughty QI Elves hewing the factual nuggets from the Mount of Tedium. Chief among the pickaxe wielders were Anne Miller, Andrew Hunter Murray, Anna Ptaszynski, Dan Schreiber and Alex Bell.

Close behind them, panning the rich silt, were Rob Blake, Will Bowen, Stevyn Colgan, Mat Coward, Jenny Doughty, Ben Dupré, Mandy Fenton, Piers Fletcher, Molly Oldfield, Justin Pollard, Liz Townsend and Rich Turner, with further gleanings from non-Elves Carla Bennett, Laura Critchley, Lauren Gilbert, Felicity J. Muth, James Phillips, Charlie Ptaszynski and Florence Schechter. And, as ever, weighing the bags of fact dust and testing their quality was Our Lady of the Wheelbarrow, the editor, Sarah Lloyd.

Finally, our grateful thanks to the wonderfully professional team at Faber: Stephen Page, Julian Loose, Anne Owen, John Grindrod and Ian Bahrami.

They're all marvellous – and that's a fact.

Index

This is here to help you find your favourite bits.
Like the facts themselves, we've kept it as simple as we can.

[315]

autobiographies 229, 254; autopsies 281; awards 308; axes 289; Aztecs 94

B&Q 89; Charles Babbage 79; babies 12, 19, 56, 94, 185, 210, 211; baby monitors 5; Baby's Bottom 102; Johannes Sebastian Bach 179; *Back to the Future* 175; bacon 263; bacteria 42, 131, 132; Bilbo Baggins 249; *Bagpuss* 31; baguette 133; John Logie Baird 56; baked beans 151; bakers 253; baldness 224; ballroom 235; balls 34; Balmoral Castle 235; Baltimore 188; bananas 160, 161; bank accounts 270; Bank of England 111, 193; bankers 305; banknotes 111; barbers 287; Barbie 282; barrel-maker 283; J. M. Barrie 105; bartender 30; baseball 17, 288; basil 173; basketball 164, 210; John Bastard 46; Mr Bastard 255; baths 18; bats 20, 44, 81, 118, 221, 262, 290; BBC 155; beach huts 249; beaks 248; beards 196, 135; bears 157; the Beatles 245, 287; bedbugs 20; beer 51, 54, 74, 107, 170, 279, 286, 304; bees 43, 118, 129, 182, 216, 221; Ludwig van Beethoven 178; Belarus 279; Belgium 5, 54, 145; Alexander Graham Bell 24; Ben Nevis 245; Berlin 289; Berlin Wall 289; Bertha 46; Bhutan 71; bicycle face 15; bicycle locks 238; Big Bang 1; Big Macs 108; bioluminescence 242; birds 132, 133, 237, 248, 272, 293; Birmingham University 14; biscuits 284; bison 144; Bitcoin 194; biting 33, 195; blackbirds 100; blankets 207; blindness 115; blood 65, 132, 279; blue 161, 101; blue whales 10, 12; blushing 27; boa constrictors 77, 113; Bodleian Library 254; body language 79; Boeing 162; Bognor Regis 61; Bolivia 116; Bollywood 19; Usain Bolt 286; bombs 1, 194; James Bond 52; bonfire night 162; books 51, 192, 227, 228, 254; Young Boozer 74; Bosnia and Herzegovina 144; bosses 270; bottoms 6, 50, 95, 157; boudoir 230; boxer shorts 5; boxing 281; Boy Scouts

243; Bra 32; Braille 202; brain surgery 116; brains 39, 65, 112, 124, 206, 248; Russell Brand 123; bras 32, 142, 222, 304; bread 240; breakfast 244; *Breaking Bad* 171; breastfeeding 296; breasts 106; breweries 74, 236; bricks 304; briefcases 246; Bristol 47; Britain 49, 162, 239, 243, 266, 302; British Library 254; broadband 8; Broadway 288; broccoli 108; Emily Brontë 95; John Buchan 301; Buckingham Palace 4; budgerigars 155; buffaloes 248; Bulgaria 50; bullets 237; bullfighting 261; bungalows 249; burgers 27, 172; burglars 142; Nicholas Burns-Cox 276; Edgar Rice Burroughs 228; buses 22, 130, 192, 266; George W. Bush 55; Kate Bush 95; bust 210; butterflies 39, 159; buttons 203; by-election 51; Lord Byron 121

cabbage patch 74; cackles 200; Julius Caesar 139; John Cage 203; cakes 240; calcium 173; California 174, 226; Caligula 139; calories 279; camels 26, 43; camembert 214; James Cameron 300; Samantha Cameron 273; can of worms 232; Canada 301; cane toads 117; cannabis 171; cannibals 63, 67; Eric Cantona 195; canyons 151; cape 228; carbon dioxide 97, 184; *carotenemia* 3; carrots 3; cars 8, 22, 115, 167, 249, 252, 298; Johnny Cash 242; cassettes 223; Butch Cassidy 30, 191; castration 224; Inês de Castro 135; catfish 66; Catherine of Aragon 164; Catherine the Great 150; Catholic Church 149; cats 93, 95, 110, 111, 113, 139, 165, 189, 263; cattle 56, 76; Catullus 84; caves 20, 21, 23, 195; caviar 232; celebrities 265; Celts 308; cemetery 240; Cerberus 264; cereal 121; chair 99; chalk 14; champagne 141, 231, 232; Charlie Chaplin 215; charioteers 213; Charles I 11; Charles II 173; cheeks 262; cheerleaders 208; cheese 63, 69, 171, 269; cheetahs 11; Chernobyl 127; Cherokee 114; chess 1, 73;

chickens 27, 125, 260; children 40, 171, 186, 299; Chile 35; chilli sauce 63; chimney sweep 153; chimpanzees 108, 277, 295; China 9, 25, 38, 53, 59, 152, 177, 178, 212, 239, 272, 305; ancient China 161, 298; chocolate 5, 126, 228; choirs 40, 166; Agatha Christie 41, 92, 93; Christmas 241; Christmas cards 54; Christmas trees 53, 138; Winston Churchill 156, 200; CIA 172; cigarettes 68; cigars 186; cinemas 242; cleavage 106; Grover Cleveland 241; climate change 153; Bill Clinton 274; clocks 116; clothing 179, 180; *Cloudy with a Chance of Meatballs* 105; coal 14; Kurt Cobain 41, 42; Coca-Cola 219; .co.ck 125; cockfighting 110; cockroaches 116; coconuts 104; codes 64; codpieces 304; coffee 37, 244; coffin 77; coins 120; Cold War 157; colds 37; Christopher Columbus 266; Colonel Sanders 254; Colorado Rapids 197; colours 119, 298; comedians 253; Commodus 220; communion wafer 232; complaints 128; computers 28, 29, 44, 46, 122, 124; condors 107, 175; Cook Islands 125; Bradley Cooper 283; *copreae* 72; copyright 156; Corby 47; Cornish 290; Corona 217; corpses 219; corrugated iron 134, 235; cough syrup 279; counterfeiters 305; *coup d'état* 198; Noël Coward 235; cowardice 298; cows 48, 117, 130, 144, 262, 290; crabs 232; craters 47; crayfish 65; crèches 185; Crewe 47; cricket 16, 117; crimes 191, 215; crisps 35, 126, 141, 142; crops 124; croquet 239; crown jewels 102; Tom Cruise 300; crying 270; Cuba 218, 281; cuddly toys 59, 309; Culloden 202; cup-and-ball (game) 73; currencies 295; Peter Cushing 138; cyberchondriacs 190; cycle paths 14; cycling 205

Puff Daddy 24; daggers 179; Roald Dahl 196, 228; *Daily Mail* 5; darkness 169; darts 103; Charles Darwin 277; dashboards 167; data 96; death 11, 18, 23, 29, 57, 85, 131, 280, 281,

[318]

exams 45; excommunication 149; excrement 305; execution 100; *The Exorcist* 83; extinction 113, 308; eye contact 286; eye shadow 148; eyeballs 12, 268; eyes 4, 43, 136

Facebook 122; faeces 108, 132; 'Fairytale of New York' 166; falafel 105; Falklands War 192, 238; Mo Farah 285; farming 124; farts 119, 272, 301; fashion 295; Michael Fassbender 283; fat 172, 184; Guy Fawkes 162; *Fawlty Towers* 84; feasts 106, 107; feathers 32, 236; Fecal Matter 42; feet 81, 106; Ferraris 230; fertility 206; FIFA 85; Fiji 38; films 35, 81, 82, 105, 242, 243; Tarquin Fin-tim-lin-bin-whim-bim-lim-bus-stop-F'tang-F'tang-Ole-Biscuitbarrel 51; fingerprints 209, 301; fingers 6, 209, 277; Finland 34, 52, 154, 269; fire engine 16; firefighters 2, 14, 174, 289; fireflies 38; Firefox 214; fireworks 161; First World War 70, 104, 137, 298; Bobby Fischer 73; fish 35, 66, 124, 271, 275; flags 230, 231; fleas 132; Ian Fleming 52; flies 97, 257; flight 21, 22, 155; flirting 275, 276; floods 70, 181, 288; flowers 292; flying pasty, delivery of 219; food 121, 124, 125; food poisoning 188; football 16, 17, 20, 85, 86, 197, 233; footprints 62; fossils 62; foxes 201, 294; France 2, 15, 70, 73, 79, 103, 176, 214, 230, 231, 270; Frankenstein's monster 34; Benjamin Franklin 7; Sigmund Freud 179; fridges 175, 199; friends 48, 49, 122, 306; frogs 80, 136, 295; Vegan Fryup 127; fuel 96; funerals 308, 309; fungi 242

Galileo 95; gambling 227; *Game of Thrones* 168; gaming 152; James Garfield 75; garlic 303; Bill Gates 284; general elections 186; genetics 33, 122; genitals 121, 128, 187; George 283; George I 280; George IV 207; Germany 17, 45, 169, 176, 229, 240, 301; gift shop 36; Gillette 196; ginger beer 74; Girl Guides 243; gladiators 82, 220; Glasgow 286; glass

136; glitter 56; global warming 37; glove puppets 175; gloves 185; glow-worms 38; glue 142; goats 139; Godzilla 65; Josef Goebbels 149; goldfish 77; golf 17, 78; Speedy Gonzalez 109; Gordon 46; gorillas 33, 203; government 79; graffiti 23, 125; ancient Greece 25, 31, 136, 240, 297; green bottles 10, 9, 8, 7, 6, 5, 4, 3, 2, 1; Graham Greene 247; Greenland 141, 151; Grenada 110; grenades 104; Grumpy Cat 284; Guantanamo Bay 36, 217; guillotining 232; guinea pigs 290; Guinness 290; guns 263, 273; gyms 226

hacking 64; haemorrhoids 301; hair 8, 37, 38, 291; Halloween 260; hallucinating 251; *Hamlet* 256; hamsters 262; hand–eye co-ordination 190; handkerchiefs 143, 297; hands 19, 37; handwriting 273; hanky-panky 213; Roger Hargreaves 299; Harley-Davidson 168; Harold I 201; harps 53; George Harrison 287; *Harry Potter* 31; Harvard University 236, 265, 266; Battle of Hastings 201; hatching 237; hats 180, 227, 241; Hawaii 139, 140, 268, 285; Stephen Hawking 95, 193; Frank Hayes 11; heart 29, 113; heartbeats 40, 221; Heathrow 87; Hebrew 105; Heineken 236; Hello Kitty 110; Ernest Hemingway 273; Henry III of France 73; hens 32; Heraclius 298; Elizabeth Hilarious 164; hippies 171; hippos 204; Emperor Hirohito 156; hissing 248; Adolf Hitler 88, 149, 150; HMS *Trident* 238; hobbits 249; Hodor Hodor; homosexuality 275, 285; honey 189; Hong Kong 253; hoopla 59; horns 39; horses 253, 255; hospitals 23, 276, 281; House of Lords 239; houses 169; Houses of Parliament 51, 278, 305; housing market 249; Victor Hugo 179; hugs 308; huh 259; humans 77, 112, 138; humming 275, 307; hummingbirds 101; humpback whales 167; hundred 244; hunger 173; Francis and Mary Huntrodd 57; hyenas 163, 200

275; Mexico 145, 217; Mexico City 267; ancient Mexico 63; MI5 241; mice 92, 263, 291; microbes 252; *Microbrachius dicki* 187; microwaves 255; Middle Ages 27; midges 257; migrations 183; Mile High Club 276; military 29, 59, 80, 236; milk 13, 48, 112, 113, 121, 144, 152, 173; Milky Way 22, 133; millionaires 245; mime 149; *Minecraft* 194; mines 193; mini golf 17; Ministry of Defence 78; Minnesota 286; Minoans 177; mistakes 23; mobile phones 6, 53, 152, 196; Mohammadabad 46; moisturiser 209; moles 88, 89; molluscs 136; Monaco 245; money 166, 246, 250, 284, 293; monkeys 119, 205; monks 33; monocles 115, 148; monorail 255; Marilyn Monroe 71; Monster Raving Loony Party 186; Monty Python 309; moon 8, 62, 78, 88, 97, 98; moonshine 98; Morse code 268; Moscow 150; mosquito nets 142; mosquitofish 99; mothers 94; Motörhead 1; motorway 14, 22, 23; mould 135; Mount Rushmore 289; mountains 118, 244; mousetraps 263; moustaches 88; mouths 126, 131; mouthwash 84; MPs 46, 123; Mr Men 299; MRI machines 183; mucus 124, 262; Robert Mugabe 208; mugs 177; mullets 16, 17; Mumbai 87; mumps 44; Murad the Cruel 224; murders 71, 139, 184; muscles 81; museums 120, 240; mushrooms 3, 4, 216, 217, 246; musical chairs 306; Benito Mussolini 241

naked boys 177; names 105, 106, 109, 114, 118, 119, 144, 171, 172, 188, 282, 283, 284; Nando's 125; nanoseconds 247; Napoleon 106, 163, 188, 228; nappies 148; narwhals 205; NASA 299, 300; national anthems 144, 145, 239; national debt 250; *National Geographic* 271; Native Americans 114; Natural History Museum 285; naughtiness 171; Nazis 238, 241; Neanderthals 20, 76; necks 158, 159; Nelson 168; nematode

worms 67; nerves 291; Netherlands 70, 71; neutrinos 133;
New Year's Eve 190; New Year's resolutions 260; New York
City 159, 183, 288, 295; New Zealand 170, 222; news 24, 155,
198; newspapers 23, 187; newsreaders 198; Isaac Newton 78;
Nicaragua 267; Jack Nicholson 73; nicknames 162; Nigeria
104; Nike 208, 234; Leonard Nimoy 229; ninjas 64; nipples
118, 215; nitrogen dioxide 184; Nokia 52; Norfolk 22, 62;
North America 113, 258; North Korea 7, 73, 74, 91; North
Pole 231; Norway 269; noses 124, 130, 131; nostrils 43,
130, 182; novels 155; *novercaphobia* 94; nuclear weapons 238;
nudity 45, 278; number plates 278; numbers 178; nuns 33;
nurses 5, 294; Nutella 299

Obama (Japan) 55; Barack Obama 114, 162; obesity 183;
oceans 97, 169, 231; octopuses 39, 296; oestrogen 303;
Oklahoma 226; Old English 157, 261; Old Mother Hubbard
255; Olympics 146, 147, 286; onesies 156; *The Onion* 196;
onions 233; opera 78; Operation Angry Birds 110; Operation
Desert Storm 148; orang-utans 203, 296; *Orange Is the New
Black* 174; orange juice 3, 290; orchestras 201; oregano 290;
organ donation 18; George Osborne 199; Oscars 175; otters
200; Oval Office 241; owls 66, 292; Oxbridge 95

Chris Packham 128; padlocks 199; pager 28; pain 166;
paint 143; Gwyneth Paltrow 284; Pancake Day 260; pandas
75; Papua New Guinea 42, 130, 233; parachutes 47, 48;
paraclausithyron 165; Paris 205; parking 185; parliament
261; Parmesan 69; particle accelerators 142; Dolly Parton
9–5, 229; passwords 64; paternity leave 233; George S.
Patton 70; PayPal 194; peanuts 10; pearls 273; pedants
123; Pelé 283; pencil sharpeners 228; penguins 66, 136;

penicillin 135, 152; penis worms 126; penises 40, 99, 197; Samuel Pepys 209; permission 270; pet food 34, 108, 111, 264; pet names 280; Peter Pan 105; Peter the Great 150; pets 111, 163; Pez 68; Philip the Good 106; phosphorescence 97; photographs 121, 271; pianos 245; pickpockets 181; picture book 51; pie charts 214; pie-eating competitions 279; pigeons 66, 71, 272, 280, 281; pigs 232, 295; pigs' bladders 143; pigtails 38; pillows 28, 150, 309; pimientos 67; Laffit Pincay Jr 10; pipes 102, 103; piracy 69; Pis-Pis 267; Brad Pitt 274; Pixar 60; pizzas 58, 164, 240; plague 27; plants 37; plastic 231; Playmobil 60; PlayStation 3 29; plutonium 1; *poecilonym* 261; poetry 29; Hercule Poirot 93; poisoning 251; Pokémon 26; poker 293; polar bears 93, 94, 296; police 110, 191; poo 43, 219, 266, 305; pool 273; 'pop' 216; pop music 61, 160, 165, 214; popcorn 35, 290; Pope John Paul II 18; popes 18, 138; porcupines 179; pornography 58, 82; porpoise 207; porridge 207; porridge, porpoise 207; Porsche 238; Portugal 135, 145, 233; postcodes 145; posters 75; Postman Pat 146; potatoes 121, 162; pouting 230; practical jokes 184; practice 237; prams 158; prayers 100; pregnancy 94, 164, 211; pretzels 33; Prince Albert 235; Prince Charles 4, 234; Prince Philip 4, 280; prisoners 174; problems 176; Prussia 201; psychologists 158; pubic lice 159; pubic wigs 138; pubs 260; pupils 259; Vladimir Putin 30; pyramids 287; pythons 272

QI 309; the Queen 4, 273, 280; Queen Victoria 24, 180, 205, 210; Quidditch 239

rabbits 218; racing 11, 285, 286; rain 104, 198, 204, 292; raspberries 38; Grigori Rasputin 30; Basil Rathbone 137;

shopping baskets 303; shopping malls 274; Shredded Wheat 63; Siberian tit 264; signatures 160; singing 40; Sinn Féin 294; sitting 99; skiing 218; skydiving 251; slaves 72, 297; sleep 90, 98, 206, 212, 294; sleepwalking 207; slinkies 307; sloths 158, 291; Slovenia 176; smallpox 207; smell 40, 87, 88, 135, 136, 303; smiling 121; Smithsonian 103; smog 115; smoking 68, 224; snails 256, 262; snakes 113, 195; sneezes 66; sniffer dogs 81; sniper 76; snooker 286; snouts 248; snow 116, 141; snowblowers 6; soap operas 19; socks 56, 92; soil 89; solar eclipses 213; solar storms 265; soldiers 27, 242; Somerset 21; songs 9, 237; soup 75, 107, 176; South Korea 90, 91; sovereign 51; space 43, 53, 90, 96, 265, 300; Spain 15, 84, 225; Spam 285; sparrows 25, 204, 215; Sparta 19, 177; species 296, 89, 91; speeding fine 52; spelling mistake 60; sperm 80, 81, 236; spiders 35, 40, 41, 62, 67, 121, 230, 257; Spock 229; sponge 239; spoonfeed 254; Spotify 9; spring 256; sprinters 130; squash 4; squids 39; squirrels 75, 195; Joseph Stalin 30, 242; *Star Wars* 242; Starbucks 172; starfish 81; stars 42; statues 286; stepmothers 94; stetsons 249; Rod Stewart 30; sticks 24; Stockholm 146; stolen 69; stomach 252; Stone Age 71; stones 182; storks 132; Barbra Streisand 73, 274; stress 37, 211, 262; students 179, 219; Luis Suárez 195; submarines 238, 255; sucking 159; 'Sucking Worm' 16; suicide 41, 70, 71; Sumatra 104; ancient Sumeria 32; sumo wrestling 281; Sun 133, 134; sunbathing 66; suntans 257; Super Bowl Sunday 36; Superman 180; supermarkets 34, 69; surnames 269; surrender 238; swarm 257; swearing 83; sweat 292, 303; Sweden 218, 269; sweet potatoes 218; sweet-and-sour sauce 107; sweets 287; swifts 294; swimming 99, 147, 181, 305; Swiss Cheese Pervert 63; Switzerland 158; synapses 248; synonym 261; Szechuan peppers 131 table tennis 4; tag 306; *A Tale of Two Cities* 141; tanks 238; tapeworms 126; tarantula hawk 129; *Tarzan* 228; taste 117, 168; tastebuds 117, 296; tattoos 72; tax 286; taxi drivers 8; tea breaks 200; teachers 72; teddy bears 75; teenagers 265; teeth 48, 49; telephones 24, 87, 187; teleportation 96; television 56, 309; temperature 133, 157, 245; David Tennant 201; tennis balls 189; *The Terminator* 300; terrapins 210; terrorism 18, 58; Tesco 69; Nikola Tesla 273; testicles 80, 176, 204, 205; testosterone 303; Texas 265; Thailand 33, 110, 215; Thames river 266; theme tunes 191; thrillers 227; thuggees 297; tick tock 167; tigers 50, 295; tightrope walking 127; time zones 258; *The Times* 197, 206; timetables 119; Titan 88; *Titanic* 91, 231; tobacco 102, 223; toenails 210; Togo 104; toilet paper 279; toilets 53, 108, 301; J. R. R. Tolkien 93; tomatoes 13, 225; Tonga 72; tongues 262; toothpaste 13; Tooting 47; *Top Gun* 59; Toronto 263; tortillas 107; tortoises 24, 107; torture 297; toupees 138; Tower of London 174; *Toy Story* 60, 175; Toyota 252; toys 24; traffic cones 286; traffic lights 115; trailers (movie) 243; trainers 208, 234; trains 116; trampolining 294; travelling 267; P. L. Travers 165; treadmills 272; trees 96, 137, 138, 302; trench foot 56; triceratops 62; Tricky 273; tricycles 205; trolleys 69; Leon Trotsky 160; trout 159; Troy 274; true or false 250; Dennis Tucker 285; tug-of-war 147; tunics 201; Turkey 75, 244; turkeys 26, 27; turnip 6; turtles 237; tusks 237; Tutankhamun 91, 92, 135; Tuvalu 250; TV licences 29; twerk 259; twins 99; Oliver Twist 30; Twister 25, 271; Twitter 96, 110, 123, 226; Tyrannosaurus rex 62

Ukraine 239; ultramarathons 253; *Ulysses* 64; umbrellas 171; umpires 288; Uncle Ben 64; unconscious 261;

underwear 143, 180; uniforms 110; United States of America
36, 42, 44, 58, 59, 63, 70, 154, 182, 218, 226, 233, 234, 236,
246, 265, 266, 278, 285, 288, 293; universe 42; Uranus 283;
urine 84, 201, 209, 241; US president 57, 75, 109, 190, 199,
241; USB sticks 81; USSR 4; Uzbekistan 45

vaginas 39; Valentine's cards 174; valet 234; Vanuatu 295;
Vatican 138; vegetarians 33, 34, 126; velvet 134; vending
machines 55; Venice 215; Venus 58, 59; *Venus de Milo* 45;
verbs 25; Vespas 252; Viagra 292; Victorians 304; Vietnam
103; Vikings 120; vinegar 82; vineyards 225; Virgin Islands
302; viruses (computer) 44; vocal cords 259; voice 40, 206;
volcanoes 7, 62, 63; vomit 55; voting 248

waffles 208; Edith Wagner 263; waist overalls 249;
waitresses 209; Wales 86; wallpaper designer 30; waltz 206;
wars 64, 70, 242; wasps 129; water 2, 3, 157, 219, 220, 292;
Watson 29; John Wayne 249; WD-40 142; weather 116;
webcams 27; websites 123, 125, 142, 300; weddings 164, 263,
278; wedgies 143; Welsh flannel 143; Bill Werbeniuk 286;
Kanye West 121; Western Front 79; whales 65, 81, 153,
291; whiskers 195; whistling 307; white 4; White House
163; Wi-Fi 162, 163; Scott Wiener 45; wigs 224; Wikipedia
123; wild boars 264; Kaiser Wilhelm II 50; William the
Conqueror 170; Robin Williams 175; Wimbledon 4, 189,
250; Winchester College 74; wind 22; wine 15, 19, 51, 54,
106, 188, 225, 228; Woking 47; wombats 163; wood 185, 289;
woodchucks 185; World Cup 197; worms 271, 272; Wright
brothers 21, 22, 162; writing 247; *Wuthering Heights* 95

Xboxes 202